# Capturing Better
# Photos & Video
# with your iPhone®

J. Dennis Thomas

WILEY

Wiley Publishing, Inc.

Capturing Better Photos and Videos with your iPhone

Published by
Wiley Publishing, Inc.
10475 Crosspoint Boulevard
Indianapolis, IN 46256
www.wiley.com

ISBN: 978-0-470-63802-6
Manufactured in the United States of America

10 9 8 7 6 5 4 3 2 1

For general information on our other products and services or to obtain technical support, please contact our Customer Care Department within the U.S. at (800) 762-2974, outside the U.S. at (317) 572-3993 or fax (317) 572-4002.

Wiley also publishes its books in a variety of electronic formats. Some content that appears in print may not be available in electronic books.

Library of Congress Control Number: 2010942337

# J. Dennis Thomas

J. Dennis Thomas is a freelance photographer and author based in Austin, Texas. He has more than 25 years of experience behind the lenses of cameras and has been using the iPhone camera since Apple first released it. His photography has been published in many regional and national publications, including *Rolling Stone, SPIN, Country Weekly*, and SXSWorld magazines.

# Credits

**Acquisitions Editor**
Courtney Allen

**Project Editor**
Jenny Brown

**Technical Editor**
Tyler Nutter

**Copy Editor**
Jenny Brown

**Editorial Manager**
Robyn Siesky

**Business Manager**
Amy Knies

**Senior Marketing Manager**
Sandy Smith

**Vice President and
Executive Group Publisher**
Richard Swadley

**Vice President and Publisher**
Barry Pruett

**Book Designer**
Erik Powers

**Media Development Project Manager**
Laura Moss

**Media Development Assistant
Project Manager**
Jenny Swisher

**Instructional Designer**
Lonzell Watson

# Acknowledgments

Thanks to all the folks at Wiley, especially Courtney, for being so patient. Thanks to Jenny and Erik for all their hard work under pressure. An extra special thanks to the crew at Thunderbird Coffee @ Manor for keeping me energized.

*For Henrietta and Maddie*
*who always make me smile…*

# Contents

Introduction . . . . . . . . . . . . . . . . . . . . . . . . . . . . . . . . . . . . . . . . . . xvii

## Chapter I - Get to Know your iPhone. . . . . . . . . . . . . . . . . . . . . . . .1

Quirks of the iPhone "Toy Camera" . . . . . . . . . . . . . . . . . . . . . . .2
Point and Shoot! . . . . . . . . . . . . . . . . . . . . . . . . . . . . . . . . . . . . . .3
All iPhones are Not Created Equal . . . . . . . . . . . . . . . . . . . . . . .4
Megapixels, Sensors and Image Quality . . . . . . . . . . . . . . . . . .6
Low Light and Digital Noise. . . . . . . . . . . . . . . . . . . . . . . . . . . .8
In Depth with Depth of Field. . . . . . . . . . . . . . . . . . . . . . . . . . .10
Shutter Lag . . . . . . . . . . . . . . . . . . . . . . . . . . . . . . . . . . . . . . . . .12
Zoom . . . . . . . . . . . . . . . . . . . . . . . . . . . . . . . . . . . . . . . . . . . . . .14
Dynamic Range . . . . . . . . . . . . . . . . . . . . . . . . . . . . . . . . . . . . .15
White Balance . . . . . . . . . . . . . . . . . . . . . . . . . . . . . . . . . . . . . .16
Getting Close . . . . . . . . . . . . . . . . . . . . . . . . . . . . . . . . . . . . . . .17
Resolution and Printing . . . . . . . . . . . . . . . . . . . . . . . . . . . . . .18

## Chapter 2 - See Like a Photographer ....................... 19

Watch for the Unusual ................................... 20

Appreciate the Ultra-Normal ........................... 21

Keep It Simple ........................................ 22

Backgrounds ......................................... 23

Color ............................................... 24

Lines, Patterns and Textures ........................... 25

Hold Steady .......................................... 26

Orientation: Portrait and Landscape .................... 27

Fill the Frame ........................................ 28

Rule of Thirds ........................................ 29

Vanishing Point ...................................... 30

Buildings and Architecture ............................. 31

Candid Shots ......................................... 32

Capture the Weather .................................. 33

Close-up and Macro ................................... 34

Pets ................................................. 35

Landscapes .......................................... 36

Travel ............................................... 37

Sunrise and Sunset .................................... 38

Wildlife ............................................. 40

## Chapter 3 - Understand the Impact of Light............ 41

Soft Light ........................................42

Indoor Lighting ..................................43

Hard Light........................................44

Outdoor Lighting.................................46

Side Lighting.....................................48

Low Light ........................................50

Back Lighting ....................................52

High Contrast ....................................54

The Golden Hour.................................56

Front Lighting....................................58

## Chapter 4 - Love the Apps.................................. 59

Adobe Photoshop Express ........................60

Plastic Bullet.....................................62

LoFi .............................................64

Diptic............................................66

Dash of Color ....................................68

FilterFX for Free......................................70

MovieFX for Free.....................................72

Camera Plus .........................................74

Gorillacam ..........................................75

Iron Camera .........................................76

Hipstamatic..........................................78

ClassicTOY - Plastic Toy Camera ......................80

moreLomo............................................82

moreMono (Red Edition)...............................84

Camera Bag..........................................86

Impression...........................................88

RetroCamera.........................................89

ShakeItPhoto.........................................90

Infinicam............................................92

Darkroom ...........................................94

Retro Camera ........................................96

Cross Process ........................................98

PanoLab............................................ 100

# Chapter 5 - Create iPhone Video..............................103

Composition........................................ 104

Keep It Sure and Steady.............................. 105

Panning ........................................... 106

Tap to Focus . . . . . . . . . . . . . . . . . . . . . . . . . . . . . . . . . . 107

Framing Heads . . . . . . . . . . . . . . . . . . . . . . . . . . . . . . . . . . 108

Mergers . . . . . . . . . . . . . . . . . . . . . . . . . . . . . . . . . . . . . . . . 109

Perspective . . . . . . . . . . . . . . . . . . . . . . . . . . . . . . . . . . . . 110

Plan your Shots . . . . . . . . . . . . . . . . . . . . . . . . . . . . . . . . . 111

Shoot Sequences . . . . . . . . . . . . . . . . . . . . . . . . . . . . . . . . 112

The Impact of Sound . . . . . . . . . . . . . . . . . . . . . . . . . . . . 113

Front Lighting . . . . . . . . . . . . . . . . . . . . . . . . . . . . . . . . . . 114

Watch for Backlighting . . . . . . . . . . . . . . . . . . . . . . . . . . 115

Trimming . . . . . . . . . . . . . . . . . . . . . . . . . . . . . . . . . . . . . 116

iMovie App . . . . . . . . . . . . . . . . . . . . . . . . . . . . . . . . . . . . 117

## Chapter 6 - Edit with Photoshop Elements 9 . . . . . . . . . . . . . 119

Quick Fix Mode . . . . . . . . . . . . . . . . . . . . . . . . . . . . . . . . 120

Full Edit Mode . . . . . . . . . . . . . . . . . . . . . . . . . . . . . . . . . 122

Cropping . . . . . . . . . . . . . . . . . . . . . . . . . . . . . . . . . . . . . . 123

Straighten Tool . . . . . . . . . . . . . . . . . . . . . . . . . . . . . . . . 124

Adjustment Layers . . . . . . . . . . . . . . . . . . . . . . . . . . . . . . 125

Levels . . . . . . . . . . . . . . . . . . . . . . . . . . . . . . . . . . . . . . . . 126

Histogram . . . . . . . . . . . . . . . . . . . . . . . . . . . . . . . . . . . . 128

Color Correction Using Levels . . . . . . . . . . . . . . . . . . . . 129

Hue and Saturation . . . . . . . . . . . . . . . . . . . . . . . . . . . . 130

Retouching . . . . . . . . . . . . . . . . . . . . . . . . . . . . . . . . . . . 132

Simulating Shallow Depth of Field . . . . . . . . . . . . . . . . 134

# Chapter 7 - Edit with iPhoto .................................. 135

Edit in Full Screen .................................... 136
The Quick Fix Tab .................................... 138
The Effects Tab ...................................... 140
Tonality and Color Adjustments ....................... 142
Photo Effects......................................... 144
The Adjust Tab ....................................... 146
Levels................................................ 148
Adjusting Tonality ................................... 150
Adjust the Details.................................... 152
White Balance........................................ 154

# Chapter 8 - Share Your iPhone Photos and Videos .......157

Download your Photos and Videos...................... 158
OS X................................................. 159

Windows . . . . . . . . . . . . . . . . . . . . . . . . . . . . . . . . . . . . . . 160

Play a Slideshow . . . . . . . . . . . . . . . . . . . . . . . . . . . . . . . . 161

E-Mail & MMS . . . . . . . . . . . . . . . . . . . . . . . . . . . . . . . . . . 162

Upload Photos and Video to Facebook. . . . . . . . . . . . . . . . 164

Send Photos and Video to Flickr . . . . . . . . . . . . . . . . . . . . 166

Upload Videos to YouTube . . . . . . . . . . . . . . . . . . . . . . . . . 168

**Chapter 9 - Accessories** . . . . . . . . . . . . . . . . . . . . . . . . . . . . . **169**

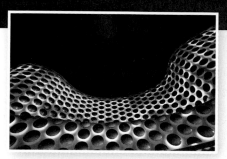

Owle Bubo . . . . . . . . . . . . . . . . . . . . . . . . . . . . . . . . . . . . . 170

Griffin Clarifi . . . . . . . . . . . . . . . . . . . . . . . . . . . . . . . . . . . 172

Gary Fong Tripod Adapter . . . . . . . . . . . . . . . . . . . . . . . . . 173

Joby Gorillamobile . . . . . . . . . . . . . . . . . . . . . . . . . . . . . . . 174

Kikkerland Jelly Lenses . . . . . . . . . . . . . . . . . . . . . . . . . . . 175

Factron Quattro Case . . . . . . . . . . . . . . . . . . . . . . . . . . . . . 176

Index . . . . . . . . . . . . . . . . . . . . . . . . . . . . . . . . . . . . . . . . . . . 177

# Introduction

Building a camera into a phone makes total sense. These days, nearly everyone carries a cell phone with them at all times; and nearly everyone owns a small digital camera to take snapshots of things that are happening in their life. So putting the two together was a no-brainer. Why carry two things when you can carry one?

A fundamental problem with most camera phones is image quality. It's often pretty bad. The sensors are incredibly tiny; the lenses aren't very good; and the range of light they can capture is pretty small … even in comparison to an inexpensive compact digital camera.

Well, the iPhone has pretty much revolutionized camera-phone photography. Of course, before the iPhone, there were other phones that had cameras built in; and now there are phones that have more advanced cameras than the iPhone has. Still, the iPhone has a cult-like following, and lots of photographers, even seasoned professionals, are using the iPhone to make great and compelling images. In fact, some iPhone photos shot with the Hipstamatic app recently ran on the front page of the *New York Times*!

Why all the fuss? Plenty of people ask why the iPhone is commanding such attention from photographers. In my opinion, the answer is short and simple: It's the apps.

The iPhone apps make the iPhone a viable instrument in photography. To be 100% honest, the camera on the iPhone isn't the greatest. The iPhone 4 has dealt with some of the issues by upgrading to a higher resolution sensor and adding the HDR option, but the camera falls short—even when compared to other phone cameras. The apps take a photo with mediocre image quality and make it cool by adding different effects. The fact that these apps are sometimes designed in part by photographers really makes a difference; oftentimes, people with no photo experience design photography software, and practical issues are not considered. Input by real photographers makes a big different. In this case, the effects are more realistic.

It bears mentioning that the best iPhone photography apps don't *hide* the shortcomings of the iPhone's camera; instead, they *add* something to a picture that makes it better. Whether it's simulating a toy camera, converting the image to black and white or sepia, adding a photo frame or other enhancement, a good app improves your iPhone photos.

This isn't to say that you need an app to make a great iPhone photo. The iPhone can and does produce some great images straight from the camera. This is where the other—more important—part of the equation comes in; that's you, the photographer. To make a good image, a scene has to be compelling. The composition, lighting and subject all have an impact on this, and these elements are all in the control of the photographer ... for the most part.

The purpose of this book is to help you develop the skills and the vision of a photographer. A lot of the concepts in this book go beyond just iPhone photography and relate to all photography. This is not only a book on how to take better pictures with your iPhone, but how to take better pictures all-around—with any type of camera. Tips on composition, lighting and subject matter are applicable to all photography.

Yet, within the coverage of general photography is specific information on how each topic relates to the iPhone ... and to the different versions of the iPhone, if there's a relevant difference among the models.

I hope this book will help you enjoy your iPhone camera even more than you already do, by giving you tips and ideas to create better photos and videos all around.

Chapter 1

# Get to Know your iPhone

As the popularity of the iPhone steadily grows, we're seeing more and more iPhone photos—everywhere. The reason for this is simple: Not everyone wants to carry around a camera, but nearly everyone has their phone with them at all times. And iPhones take decent photos.

Many people, even professional photographers (including me), rely on an iPhone to catch everyday snapshots and to make great images on the fly. Although the quality of photos made with a cell phone camera, like the iPhone, isn't nearly as high as those made with a DSLR ... or even a good compact camera, your iPhone has the advantage of easy access.

*Figure 1-1* *A Holga is a toy camera that is known for soft focus and vignetting. I used the iPhone's Camera Bag app "Helga" setting to simulate a Holga-type image.*

# Quirks of the iPhone "Toy Camera"

The iPhone camera lens isn't top quality. There's no optical zoom or image stabilization; the images can be very grainy and even blurry; and highlights are often blown out. Despite these flaws, there is a cultish following of people who just love to take pictures with an iPhone. You're probably wondering why. Well, the reason is that we iPhone photographers use the shortcomings of the iPhone camera to our advantage.

If you're familiar with photography at all, you may have heard the term *toy camera*. This term refers to cheap mass-produced cameras such as the Holga and Lomo. These cameras have quirks due to the cheap nature of the materials used to manufacture them. But these quirks are exactly why some photographers like to use them. They can make fun art photos.

This is how I view my iPhone camera—as a toy camera. Interestingly enough, there are many iPhone apps that actually simulate the effect of the Holga and Lomo cameras.

This book is written to help you learn the quirks and foibles of the iPhone camera as well as some key photographic techniques. This will help you grow as a photographer and inspire you to make some really great and interesting works of art with your iPhone.

*Figure 1-2 Making an interesting composition is the key to point-and-shoot photography. This image was processed using Plastic Bullet.*

# Point and Shoot!

*Point and Shoot* is sort of a slang term in the photography world that refers to small, easily controlled compact cameras that are generally used by non-photographers to capture snapshots of friends and family. By definition, many of the cameras that are described as "point and shoot" aren't really point-and-shoot cameras, because there are lots of settings you can change on them, such as shutter speed, aperture, ISO and more.

The iPhone, however, is a true point and shoot unit. There are no settings you can adjust. Literally all you can do is *point* and *shoot*. With the iPhone 3Gs and 4, you can pick a point of focus in an image by tapping the area on the screen, and this gives you a little more creative control than the previous versions of iPhone. But that's all you'll get with this camera.

Therefore, with a true point-and-shoot iPhone camera in hand, you will find that it's up to you to seek out great subjects and optimal lighting and to use your creativity to make interesting compositions and truly great images.

# All iPhones are Not Created Equal

Since the first iPhone rolled out to market, there have been many improvements. Most of the advances have enhanced the phone quality and the apps' functionality and selection, but Apple has also made quite a few changes to the camera as well. For this reason, not every iPhone has the same photography and videography capabilities.

Of course, the new generation iPhones have the most advanced technology. But Apple offers some upgrades to cameras with iOS 4.

The iPhone 3Gs and 4 enable the use of a digital zoom to allow you to get visually closer to far-off subjects. This option is now available for the 3G and phones with the iOS 4 upgrade. We'll cover the zoom feature in more detail later in this chapter.

As I mentioned previously, the iPhone 3Gs (with iOS 4 upgrade) and the iPhone 4 allow you to select a focus point in an image by tapping the area. That is, by tapping a spot in an image, you tell the camera to focus there. In the work of photography, this is knows as *selective focus*, and it is one of the most powerful tools available to photographers. It's used to direct the viewer's eye to a certain feature or specific area of your image.

One new feature that is available only with the iPhone 4 is the LED flash. This feature shines a bright light on your subject to help you get sharper and clearer image in low-light situations. By default, the flash is set to come on automatically in low light, but a quick tap can turn it off.

I prefer to leave this set to "Off" and to use the flash only if it's absolutely necessary. In some situations, the flash can make an image look very unnatural, and the light can be quite unflattering for your subjects, especially when shooting portraits. When your subject is backlit though (that is, when the light source is behind the subject), the flash can help to fill in the shadows and thereby balance the lighting in front of and behind your subject.

**Figure 1-3** *Using the flash can give you a sharper picture; but not using flash makes your picture look more natural. The shot on the left used flash. The image on the right was taken with available light.*

# Megapixels, Sensors and Image Quality

The most notable improvement in the various models of iPhone is the increase in resolution. The original iPhone screen was two megapixels, and the 3G was upgraded to three megapixels with the 3Gs. Resolution jumped up to five megapixels with the iPhone 4.

More megapixels results in improved resolution. High resolution means that images and graphics on the screen are sharper and clearer than those viewed at a low resolution. But as always, there's no free lunch.

While there are more pixels added with each upgrade, the physical size of the sensor in the iPhone remains the same, making each pixel smaller. So each pixel is less effective at gathering light than in phones with fewer pixels available. Ironically, this means that cameras with higher resolutions perform worse in low light situations than those with lower resolutions.

Fortunately, Apple compensated for this in the iPhone 4 by including a rather new technology called *Backside Illumination*, or BSI.

Image sensors are built-in layers. For standard illuminated sensors, the photons of light pass through a camera lens and are directed through micro-lenses that are situated on top of each pixel. The photons then pass through a thin layer of metal wiring before ultimately finding their way to the photo diode, which collects the photons and converts them into electrons that can be deciphered by an Analog to Digital converter before ultimately ending up as image data.

What BSI does is switch the order of the layers so that the wiring is underneath the photo-diodes. This allows the photons direct access, so that less light is lost. The sensor in this setup is much more effective at collecting light; therefore, it can perform better when the light is low.

What it boils down to is this: Although the iPhone 4 has more pixels jammed into the same sized sensor as the previous iPhones, it has comparable, although slightly better, low-light capabilities.

Don't worry if you're not among those with an iPhone 4. All versions of the iPhone are very capable of capturing great photos, especially in well-lit situations.

**Figure 1-4** *Thanks to BSI, the iPhone 4 can take clean pictures in low light.*

*Figure 1-5* *You can see the colored specks of digital noise in this image.*

# Low Light and Digital Noise

As previously mentioned, the iPhone is known to do perform well, but not great, in low light.

This doesn't mean that images are blurry when it gets dark (although this can happen), but the images suffer from excessive *noise*. Noise is a term that describes artifacts that appear in images when shot in low light. These artifacts add a grainy look to the image.

Noise appears as random colored speckles throughout an image and is usually more noticeable in the shadow areas. Noise is the by-product of turning up the gain of the image sensor to make it more sensitive to light. This adjustment to the image sensor allows you to shoot in low light without having prohibitively long shutter speeds.

Interestingly enough, the original iPhone actually performs better in low light than either the 3G or the 3Gs … most likely because of the better light-gathering capabilities of the larger pixels in the sensor.

Unfortunately, you can't control how sensitive the iPhone sensor is, so you're pretty much stuck with noise in your images if you decide to shoot in low light. The only way to really reduce the noise in these images is to use some sort of noise-reduction technology when post-processing.

***Figure 1-6*** *Your best bet for cleaning up low-light images is to use the noise reduction feature in Photoshop or iPhoto.*

***Figure 1-7*** *PhotoTidy is a free app that does an okay job at reducing noise in your low-light iPhone shots.*

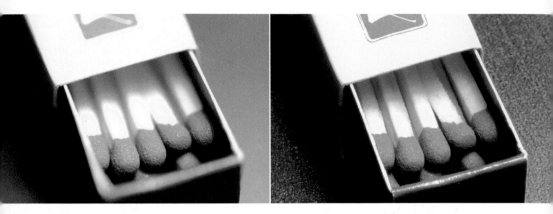

*Figure 1-8* *These shots were taken with a DSLR to show the extreme differences in depth of field that can be achieved with the right gear.*

# In Depth with Depth of Field

Depth of field is a tricky concept to explain, but it's easy to understand once you see it. Technically defined, depth of field is the area in an image that is acceptably sharp to the human eye.

In traditional photography, opening and closing the aperture of the lens controls the depth of field in an image. The lens aperture acts like the iris of the eye. It opens and closes to control the amount of light that is allowed in.

Photographers use depth of field to determine how much of a scene is in focus. You use a shallow depth of field to isolate the subject from the background. A deep depth of field ensures that everything in the image is in focus.

Of course you've probably already guessed that you can't adjust the aperture of the lens on your iPhone. (The aperture is fixed at f/2.8). So it's good to know that aside from aperture, two other features have an effect on depth of field; they are focus distance and sensor size.

Being that the sensor in the iPhone is very small, achieving a truly shallow depth of field with this camera is quite difficult. But since the focus distance also affects depth of field, you have a rudimentary way to control depth of field with the iPhone 3Gs and 4. Here it is: If you stand close it your subject, the depth of field of your image will be more shallow than if you stand farther away.

**Figure 1-9** *Focusing on the subject close-up allowed me to get a shallow depth of field.*

# Shutter Lag

One of the things I find most irritating about any camera phone, iPhone included, is shutter lag. This is the term used to describe the time between pressing the shoot button (or, in the case of the iPhone, tapping the camera icon) and when the picture is actually taken.

In a lot cases, if you're taking a picture of a landscape or shooting a portrait, the shutter lag isn't a major problem. But try to take a picture of a quickly moving subject, where timing is important, and you'll see what I mean.

Basically, a long shutter lag makes shooting sports with the iPhone kind of tricky. You can easily catch a moving subject; but catching the peak of the action is sometimes very difficult—unless you can anticipate it and shoot early. The shutter lag on the original iPhone and the iPhone 3G is pretty bad; sometimes it is as much as one whole second. The 3Gs and the iPhone 4 are much quicker.

**Figure 1-10**  *In this photo, you can see that I missed the peak of the action due to shutter lag.*

> **Hint:** *The iPhone doesn't release the shutter until you pull your finger off of the screen. To more accurately time your shutter release, press and hold on the screen until you want to shoot.*

**Figure 1-11**  *Here, I actually caught the peak of the action, but it took a few tries.*

*Figure 1-12* *I used the 5X digital zoom to capture this image of my dog Maddie. Notice that the digital zoom causes the image to appear mottled and out of focus.*

# Zoom

The iPhone 4, 3Gs and 3G (with iOS 4) enable a feature called *digital zoom*. Basically this feature crops into the image area and simulates the effect of an optical zoom lens, which brings a viewer closer to your subject.

The problem with digital zoom is that it diminishes resolution. The more you zoom in, the more image quality declines. I almost never use this feature due to the poor picture quality it produces, so I recommend that you use it sparingly … if at all.

Instead of zooming, you can usually get better results by cropping the image using Photoshop Elements or iPhoto after you have downloaded it to your computer. Find more information on these image-editing tools in Chapters 6 and 7.

**Figure 1-13** *Images with very bright areas often lose detail in iPhone-shot photos. In extreme cases, ultra bright areas appear as pure white. This is referred to as blown out highlights. Avoid blown out highlights by focusing on the brightest part of a scene.*

# Dynamic Range

*Dynamic Range* is a term that refers to the span between highlights and shadows (lights and darks) that a digital sensor can capture. DSLRs have a fairly high dynamic range, which means that this type of camera can capture a very broad span of luminosities—from deep shadows to bright whites and all of the tones in between.

Unfortunately, the iPhone sensor isn't known to be the best when it comes to capturing a wide spectrum of brightness. Although the iPhone 4 is much improved over the earliest versions of the iPhone, it still doesn't compare to a DSLR or even most compact cameras. This is why you'll often notice that the brightest areas in an iPhone-shot image are completely blown out (solid white), especially in high contrast images.

This happens because the iPhone is trying to capture detail in the shadow areas … at the expensive of retaining detail in the highlights. Your best bet for dealing with this is to avoid scenes with a lot of contrast and a wide range of lights and darks. A good example of a scene to avoid is a bright sunny day at high noon with deep shadows.

*Figure 1-14* *The picture on top shows how the iPhone set the white balance. I used iPhoto to adjust the white balance to give the picture a more natural look.*

# White Balance

All light sources emit light of a different color. As humans, we are lucky that our brains adjust to the different color temperatures and allow us to see white as white. Our camera sensors are different. They see colors as an absolute. So in order to render a scene as neutral, the White Balance setting often needs to be adjusted.

As you've probably guessed by now, the iPhone adjusts the white balance automatically, so there's nothing you can do in the way of setting it. You're stuck with the Auto White Balance setting of the iPhone. But fortunately, if the white balance looks off in your images, you can always adjust it using post-processing software.

*Figure 1-15* I used a Kikkerland close up jelly lens to take this extreme macro shot of a 20 pence coin. This image was processed using the Infinicam app.

# Getting Close

All lenses have a minimum focus distance, and the iPhone is no exception. The *minimum focus distance* refers to the smallest distance between you and a subject that a camera will allow while still achieving focus.

The original iPhone and the iPhone 3G have a minimum focus distance of about eight inches, which doesn't really allow you to get very good close-up shots. The iPhone 3Gs and the iPhone 4 can focus much closer, down to about two inches.

If you want to get closer focus with the original iPhone or the 3G, there are a couple of accessories you can get. I suggest that you check out the Kikkerland close up jelly lens.

# Resolution and Printing

A lot of folks like to print their photos. It's a great way to show off your camera-work to friends and co-workers. And most people like to display their photography work at home and work. Photo prints also make great gifts. Using your own work allows you to add a more personal touch than buying a picture from the mall.

So keep these tips in mind when printing. It'll help you get the show- and gift-worthy images you envision.

*Figure 1-16* *iPhone photo prints make great gifts.*

The size of your printed image is limited by the resolution of the photo file, which is expressed in megapixels. The number of megapixels is calculated by multiplying the number of individual pixels ... length by width. If you print images bigger than the size that the resolution dictates, you'll get photos that look extremely pixilated (i.e., "dotty") and fuzzy.

The original iPhone and the 3G share the same sensor, which offers a resolution of two megapixels (1200x1600). The 3Gs has a resolution of 3.2 megapixels (1536x2048), and the iPhone 4 has an impressive five megapixels (1944x2592).

Most commercially available photo printers print at a resolution of 240 dpi. To figure out the maximum size that you can print, divide the number of pixels by 240. So, for example, say you have an iPhone 3G. Take 1200 and divide it by 240 ($1200 \div 240 = 5$). This means that five inches is the maximum height or width of your print showing your iPhone 3G photo.

iPhone and iPhone 3G max print is 5x6.5 (or 5x7)
iPhone 3Gs max print is 6.4x8.5 (or 6x9)
iPhone 4 max print is 8.1x10.8 (or 8x10)

Keep in mind that if you crop your images, your print size will need to decrease as well.

## Chapter 2

# See Like a Photographer

The key to taking great photos and making cool art with your iPhone actually has nothing to do with the iPhone at all. The key is YOU! When you learn how to think like a photographer, your images will start improving each time you use your camera. And soon, you won't even think about it; skilled shooting will become second nature.

Professional photographers follow many different rules … *guidelines* really … when creating images. None of these guidelines/ rules are mandatory—or even appropriate in all situations. Sometimes you need to break a rule or two to get the greatest impact out of your shot.

This chapter is full of all kinds of tips and tricks that I've picked up in my twenty-odd years of working behind a camera. From composition techniques to pointers on how to get specific shots, the tips in this chapter can help you start thinking like a photographer.

*Figure 2-1* I snapped this shot of the mythical Jackalope at a BBQ place in Lockhart, Texas.

# Watch for the Unusual

Some of the most compelling photographs are those in which the subject is odd, off-kilter … or sometimes just plain weird. Keep your eyes open for the out-of-the-ordinary visuals you're lucky enough to experience. Look for things that are out of place, like a flower sprouting out of urban decay.

**Figure 2-2** *This close-up shot of some colorful bracelets at a vendor's stand are a bright and sparkly example of everyday objects.*

## Appreciate the Ultra-Normal

Don't get so caught up in looking for weird things that you forget about the appeal of everyday objects. Beauty lies everywhere … even in the things you see all the time.

Take a moment to look at your surroundings. Interesting things sometimes hide right out in the open. Noticing the details in a kitchen utensil or neighborhood mailbox can yield cool results.

*Figure 2-3  Having just one simple subject makes your images more captivating to the viewer.*

# Keep It Simple

One of the easiest rules of photography to remember is "Keep it simple." And it's an important one.

When a photo is cluttered, viewers can have a tough time figuring out what the subject is, and this lessens the impact of the image. Keep your images simple to allow the subject to stand out.

# Backgrounds

Sometimes people get so focused on a subject that they forget to look at the background. Especially when shooting with a camera like the iPhone, it's imperative to consider the background of a scene if you want your images to be great. The iPhone camera has a deep depth of field, so the background is almost always in focus.

Simple backgrounds work best with most subjects, but sometimes you need to include objects in the background to give a sense of place. For example, if you're in France, it's a great idea to have the Eiffel Tower in the background. But if you're taking a simple portrait, then a plain colored wall might be your best bet. Busy backgrounds can draw the viewer's eye from your subject.

*Figure 2-4  The busy background detracts from the main subject of this quick portrait of my nephew Seamus.*

One major thing to look for in a background are *mergers*—things that look like they're sprouting from a person's head or shoulders. (Think of a tree that looks like it's growing straight out of granny's head when you look at the picture of her at the park.) Mergers are generally to be avoided unless you intentionally add them for comic value.

*Figure 2-5* *Use complementary colors to add interest to your subject.*

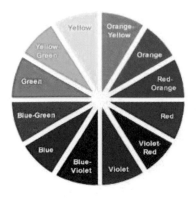

# Color

Bright, bold, outlandish colors make for great images—that stand out from the pack. Complementary colors are always a good bet as well. When complementary colors are placed next to each other, they appear brighter and can help hold the viewer's attention by adding interest or a dynamic tension to the scene.

On the color wheel, complementary colors are shown directly opposite each other.

The orange / red-hued colors of this apartment building stand out against the deep blue of the sky and create a great contrasting image.

*Figure 2-6* *The road creates an S-curve in this shot.*

*Figure 2-7* *The bold vertical lines create a dynamic tension in this shot.*

# Lines, Patterns and Textures

Lines in an image help to lead the eyes into the picture. The S-curve is often used in photographic images to lead a viewer's eyes through the scene. Diagonal and straight lines work great, too.

Bold patterns always make dynamic images. Keep an eye out for strong repetitive designs. These can be man-made as well as naturally occurring.

Textures can be used to give viewers a tactile feeling when looking at your images. The smoothness of a pile of pebbles, the rough asphalt on a badly maintained road or a lizard's scales are all good subjects for introducing textures into an image.

# Hold Steady

There're few things worse than a blurry image. When the light gets dark, shutter speeds slow down and it gets more difficult to get sharp images. Keeping your iPhone steady when shooting, especially in low-light situations, is imperative.

I use a couple of different techniques to keep the camera steady. First, when holding the iPhone to take a picture, keep your elbows tight to your sides. Holding the iPhone out at arm's length can introduce shake. Sometimes, if the light is really low, I'll set the iPhone on a stable surface.

There are also apps that can help. One such app is Darkroom, which uses the accelerometer to determine when the camera is steady before it snaps the photo.

There are also tripods that are made to hold your iPhone if you like to shoot in the dark.

*Figure 2-8* I used the Darkroom app to help get a sharp image in a relatively low-light situation.

# Orientation: Portrait and Landscape

There are two ways in which you can orient your photos: Portrait and Landscape. These terms refer to the alignment that is most commonly used with the respective types of photography. *Landscape* orientation is horizontal; the long sides are on the top and bottom. *Portrait* orientation is vertical and has the short sides on the top and bottom.

Now, by no means are you stuck with using portrait orientation for a portrait or landscape with a landscape. Many great portraits have been shot in landscape orientation and vice-versa.

The point of this tip is "Try it both ways." With every subject, try shooting one each way. You never know which way will work best, and sometimes you'll be surprised with the results. It only takes a second to get another shot, and it may mean the difference between capturing a good image and a really great one.

*Figure 2-9* *This landscape shot was taken in portrait orientation.*

***Figure 2-10*** *Getting close to your subject helps to fill the frame and avoid dead space in your images.*

# Fill the Frame

This is an oft-overlooked guideline for composition. Most snapshots feature the subject somewhat lost in a vast space. This leaves room for lots of clutter and competing elements in an image that vie for viewer attention.

Avoid this by moving closer to your subject and filling the frame with your intended focal point. This gives viewers no doubt as to what the subject is, which makes for a more interesting photo.

*Figure 2-11* *The dome of the Texas State Capitol is placed*
*off to the side in accordance with the Rule of Thirds.*

# Rule of Thirds

I think this is one of the most important rules in photography and art in general. Most non-photographers simply place the subject smack-dab in the middle of the frame and snap the shot. While this makes for decent snapshots and gets the point across, the goal here is to take *better* photos. Stray from the middle sometimes.

The easiest way to take better photos is to make them more interesting. The quickest way to make a photo more interesting is to use dynamic subject placement through the Rule of Thirds.

To understand the Rule of Thirds, imagine that your image area is divided into thirds (think tic-tac-toe). Placing a subject on or near one of the intersections gives an image a more dynamic feel, and this subconsciously makes it more interesting to the viewer.

*Figure 2-12* *The lines of the highway end in a vanishing point.*

# Vanishing Point

The point at which parallel lines seem to converge in a scene is the *vanishing point*. Using a vanishing point in your images provides leading lines that draw a viewer's eyes through the image. It also gives the image a sense of depth.

# Buildings and Architecture

Some of the most difficult things to shoot with the iPhone are buildings. Not that it's difficult to point the camera at a building and press the button; the problem lies with *perspective*.

By standing close to a building and shooting up at it, you create an illusion that the building is tipping over. If you're going for this type of look, then great. If not, you need to adjust your perspective.

The best way to deal with this problem is to move back from the building to put some distance between it and you. Distance lessens the impact of perspective distortion.

Another solution is to use a program such as Photoshop to manipulate the images in post-processing. If you plan on editing the images, be sure to leave plenty of space around the sides of the frame to accommodate the loss of some image area, which will occur as the image is stretched to correct the distortion.

**Figure 2-13** *Stepping back and shooting this building from across the street lessened the impact of perspective distortion.*

*Figure 2-14* *I snapped this candid shot of my bass player Chris while we were taking a break from recording in the studio. The image was processed with the Sloppy Borders app.*

# Candid Shots

Candid shots are photos that are snapped at the spur of a moment. They are unplanned and happen as a moment unfolds. Don't spend too much time composing a candid photo or you'll lose the shot as the moment passes.

One tip for a great candid is to capture action. Photos of people *doing* something are much more interesting than people sitting still.

Great times to take candid shots are during family get-togethers or when you're hanging out with friends. A lot of people like to capture candid shots of strangers while they are out around town; but this can annoy some people. So proceed with caution if you intend to do that kind of photography (also known as *street photography*).

**Figure 2-15** *This picture of a tree losing its leaves evokes a feeling of autumn. The image was processed with the Plastic Bullet app.*

# Capture the Weather

If there's one thing you can count on being available to photograph, it's the weather. There will always be *some* sort of weather … whether it's sunny or raining or snowing. A nice snowy landscape or an ominous shot of a thunderstorm blowing in are always crowd pleasers. But peaceful sunny days can also be good. The key here is capturing the essence and feeling of the weather.

*Figure 2-16* *I used the close-focus capabilities of the iPhone 4 to take this shot of a butterfly.*

# Close-up and Macro

Close-up and macro photography involves getting very near your subject to bring out the details. The iPhone 3Gs and the iPhone 4 have a close-focusing capability, so you can try your hand at close-ups right out of the box.

As mentioned before, the original iPhone and the iPhone 3G are not very adept at the close-up shots, but don't worry. There are accessories you can buy that will allow your iPhone lens to focus super-close. There are also DIY methods.

Some people use small pocket magnifying lenses to get close ups with an iPhone. Just hold the magnifying glass in front of the camera lens or use lenses from a DVD player that you no longer use.

Griffin makes a case for the 3G that has a built-in magnifying lens as well; it's called the Clarifi. Personally, I use the Kikkerland Jelly Lens for close-ups.

One thing to be aware of when attempting close-up photography is that the closer you focus on something, the more pronounced camera shake will be in your photo. So be sure to hold the camera very still to get a nice sharp close-up.

*Figure 2-17  Pets make great photography subjects.*
*This image was processed using the Camera Bag app.*

# Pets

Our pets (and other people's pets, too) offer some of the best photo ops. Try to capture your pet's personality when you take his/ her photo.

Shoot from your pet's eye level sometimes. We can get so used to looking down at our pets that we forget to get down to their level. Doing so can make a more intimate portrait. Shooting down at them from a standing position can still result in a great photo though, as some of my favorite shots of my dogs are of them looking up at me.

Have some treats handy or make funny noises to get your pet to look at you.

*Figure 2-18* *I placed the horizon line at the bottom third of the image, following the Rule of Thirds.*

# Landscapes

Landscapes are a very traditional type of photography and they are a great way to remember the places you've been. These shots are also great talking points when showing your friends different places.

It's a good idea to follow the Rule of Thirds when composing a landscape. That means placing the horizon line either at the top or bottom third of the composition. You rarely want to place the horizon in the center, although in some cases in can work quite well. You'll just need to use your creative eye to make the call on this. Or, shoot a landscape using a few different positions for the horizon and see which one you like best.

The best time to shoot a landscape is early morning or early evening, when the sun is low in the sky. This is when the light is most beautiful. It results in rich, glowing, colored skies and soft directional light.

# Travel

Travel photography is a broad term. It can be anything from candid shots of locals and pictures of the terrain to photos of an area's architecture.

Travel photography is all about capturing the essence of the places through which you travel. Interesting people, cool buildings and general scenery are all things to capture.

The best tip I can give here is to shoot *everything*. Take a lot of photos, so that you don't miss anything. You may end up with a lot of shots that you have to sort through and edit, but it's better to have shot something when travelling and not like the image than to have not taken the picture and regret it later.

**Figure 2-19** *This photo was shot at a popular surf spot in Encinitas, California. The foreign-looking architecture contrasts with the surfing sign, which makes for an interesting travel shot.*

# Sunrise and Sunset

Sunrise and sunset photos can be some of the most gorgeous photos you can capture. The deep saturated colors of the sky—created by the bending of the sun's rays by the atmosphere—make for some really dynamic images.

Unfortunately, due to the limited dynamic range of the iPhone sensor and the inability to set the exposure, these types of shots can be a little difficult to achieve with the iPhone.

To control the metering, so that the iPhone doesn't blow out the highlights, it's best to focus right on the brightest part of the image.

With the original iPhone and the iPhone 3G, this means placing the sun right in the middle of the image area. This will cause the iPhone to expose

*Figure 2-20* Tapping focus on the brightest part if the sky helped me get a silhouette of the palm tree.

for the brightest part of the image, underexposing the shadows to produce saturated colors. The iPhone 3Gs and 4 allow you to choose the focus point, so you can be a little more flexible with your compositions.

The landscape composition tips on the previous page also apply here.

**Figure 2-21** *Having my iPhone handy allowed me to capture a nice sunrise along a west Texas highway.*

*Figure 2-22* *Semi-tame animals like this duck are pretty easy to snap photos of with your iPhone.*

# Wildlife

Photographing wildlife with the iPhone isn't quite the same as photographing wildlife with a DSLR, but you can do it. Generally, wildlife photographers head out into the wilderness with long telephoto lenses to capture elusive wild animals from a great (i.e., safe) distance.

With the iPhone, you're more likely to be capturing images of semi-tame animals in the wilds of an urban setting or rural farm than in the true wilderness. The zoo is a great place to grab some "wildlife" shots. You may need to use the zoom feature, but as I warned before: It's a good idea to use the zoom sparingly, because it degrades your images quite quickly. To enlarge your subject, think about cropping in post processing instead.

Another place to catch wildlife is your local park or backyard. Often you can get close enough to a bird or squirrel to snap a good close-up shot.

If you're really keen on catching some animals that are far off, there are telephoto lens accessories that attach to your iPhone. Search for "iPhone telephoto accessories" on the Internet to find a myriad of options in different price ranges.

# Chapter 3

# Understand the Impact of Light

Light is a fundamental element of photography. Understanding the impact that light has on your subject and overall scene is pivotal to your ability to create excellent pictures.

Light has different qualities that play important roles in the presentation of your photo to viewers. The *quality of light* in an image impacts what a viewer sees and it guides how they perceive the visual you're presenting. Likewise, the *direction of light*, as it illuminates a subject, also has a huge impact on how the subject looks. This also matters a great deal to the quality of your images.

With a sharp eye and a little planning, you'll be able to find the right light in almost any situation, and this will help you make the best images possible with your iPhone camera.

*Figure 3-1* *A cloudy day offers a nice soft light to this quick portrait.*

# Soft Light

Soft light is also known in the photography world as *diffused light*. By far, this is the most desirable type of lighting for just about any subject. It has little contrast and is therefore much more friendly to the sensor in your iPhone than bright light that produces harsh shadows (described next). Remember, the iPhone doesn't handle high-contrast situations very well.

A broad or large light source provides the softest light. This type of light soothes textures by seemingly wrapping around the subject and filling in the shadows.

Some examples of soft lighting include cloudy days and window lighting. You can also move your subject into a shaded area out of the direct sun to get soft light for a photo.

*Figure 3-2* A simple lamp provided the light for this portrait of local photographer Tim Pipe.

# Indoor Lighting

Shooting photos indoors can be tricky. Available light from overhead bulbs can be harsh. But by moving a lamp closer to your subject when indoors, you can make the light source larger in relation to the subject and thereby soften the light.

One of the best ways to get soft light indoors, especially for a portrait, is to position the subject in front of a large, bright window that isn't receiving direct sunlight. The *window light* portrait is very popular with many professional photographers. This is a very simple trick that will make your portraits stand out and flatter your subject(s).

One thing to be aware of when taking pictures indoors is that different types of light bulbs have different color temperatures. The iPhone attempts to neutralize the effect by adjusting the white balance, but it is not always successful.

*Figure 3-3* *Bright hard sunlight is great for shooting plants and flowers.*

# Hard Light

Hard light is very directional. It casts distinct shadows and has much more contrast than soft light.

Compared with soft lighting, the light source for hard light is small in relation to the subject. Moving a light away from a subject makes the light harder.

The best example of a hard light source is the sun. Although, technically speaking, it is massive and certainly not close to a subject. But at about 93 million miles away,

**Figure 3-4** *Hard lighting makes for dramatic portraits, such as this one of photographer Jay West.*

the sun is a relatively small-sized light source compared to subjects on Earth, and it creates very harsh lighting situations.

In photography, hard lighting is used to highlight texture and it can create an air of mystery in a portrait.

When hard light is your only option, try to keep the sun at your back. This means your subject will be lit from the front and you can easier avoid an underexposed subject.

*Figure 3-5* *A cloudy sky made for a nice soft-light portrait of my friend Megan. This image was processed with the Polarize app.*

# Outdoor Lighting

Usually the best scenario for taking pictures outdoors is on a partly cloudy day. When the sun is hidden behind a cloud, the cloud diffuses the light, making it much softer.

An easy way to get soft light when outdoors on a sunny day is to move to a shaded area. Under a porch, veranda or overhang is ideal. Be aware of your background though; if it's too bright, you will have blown-out areas that can be distracting.

If you move your subject under a shade tree, watch out for mottling. This happens when sunlight shines between the leaves and hits the subject, causing spots of extreme bright areas.

**Figure 3-6** *I used an umbrella to diffuse the bright sunlight for this portrait of my niece J'Ana.*

*Figure 3-7* *Side lighting makes a two-dimensional photo look three-dimensional!*

# Side Lighting

Place your subject so that light hits it from an angle. This creates a much more dynamic and dramatic lighting scenario than front lighting. Side lighting adds some shadows and brings out contour, which add an illusion of depth to photos.

*Figure 3-8* *The texture of the wall is highlighted by side lighting.*

**Figure 3-9** *For this night shot of Dirty Martin's hamburger joint in Austin, Texas, I used an adapter that allowed me to attach the iPhone to a standard tripod.*

# Low Light

One of the biggest obstacles to overcome with iPhone photography is getting good photos in low-light situations. To do so requires the use of higher sensitivity settings, which adds noise to your images. In low light, the iPhone also uses longer shutter speeds, which can cause your images to be blurry.

To combat blurry images from longer shutter speeds, you can use a tripod to stabilize the iPhone to help your images look sharp. A simpler, although less effective, option is to stabilize your body by leaning against something solid like a light pole. Keeping your elbows in close to your body also helps to minimize shake.

*Figure 3-10*  *I used a light pole to help me stabilize the iPhone to get a sharp shot of the New York, New York Casino in Las Vegas. Effects were added to this image with Photoshop.*

**Figure 3-11** *Placing the sun behind the dinosaur added a nice halo effect to this photograph. The image was processed using the LoFi app.*

# Back Lighting

Back lighting is a tricky situation. It will often ruin your photos by introducing flare and lowering contrast. But sometimes, for the same reasons, it can make your images much more interesting.

The key is to find the right placement of the light source. Blocking the light source with the subject is a good way to get a usable backlit shot like this photo of a roadside attraction in Cabazon, California.

**Figure 3-12** *Backlighting provides an interesting flare to this photo of my Boston Terrier, Maddie. This image was processed using the MoreLomo app.*

*Figure 3-13* *This is the original photo of the Flamingo Hotel in Las Vegas. Notice the blown-out highlights.*

# High Contrast

Another challenge for iPhone photographers is high contrast. Scenes with bright sunlight and strong shadows—as well as dark scenes with brightly lit areas—are two common high contrast scenes.

The iPhone camera's sensor just isn't capable of capturing details in both dark shadows and bright areas. Therefore, high contrast scenes often translate to images that have completely white areas with no detail. These are known as *blown out* areas.

**Figure 3-14** *This photo shows the HDR version from the iPhone 4. Notice that the details in the highlight and shadow areas are much more clear.*

To deal with this problem, Apple added an HDR feature to the camera with iOS 4.1. This takes three photos almost simultaneously and outs them together to increase the detail in both the light and dark areas of the picture.

If your phone doesn't have this feature, it's best to just avoid high contrast scenes. Or, try moving your subject into an area with less contrast.

You can also download the Pro HDR app, which provides the same functionality as the HDR feature built into iOS 4.

*Figure 3-15* *This landscape photo was taken at the golden hour in White Sands, New Mexico.*

## The Golden Hour

This is a term that photographers often use to describe the period of time just after sunrise and just before sunset. The golden hour is so called because the light at these times is being refracted through the atmosphere, and this produces a beautiful golden light.

The golden hour is an especially great time to take landscape shots, architectural photos and portraits.

There's actually an iPhone app called the Golden Hour. It tells you exactly when the golden hour is … anywhere in the world.

*Figure 3-16* *A shot of the Frost Bank building in Austin, Texas, at the golden hour.*

**Figure 3-17** *Good old-fashioned front lighting was used for this detail shot of the controls of an old tower clock.*

# Front Lighting

There's an old photography adage that goes, "Keep the sun at your back." This is a pretty good rule to follow when taking snapshots. When your subject is lit from the front, you usually capture nice, even and flat lighting.

Although front lighting works reasonably well for a lot of subjects, it can sometimes lack depth. Turning your subject slightly away from the light source can help to add a little depth to your front-lit photo.

## Chapter 4

## Love the Apps

One of the coolest things about iPhone photography is that … with apps … you can do so many different things. There are apps that apply special effects; apps that allow you to crop, boost saturation and make other post processing edits; and there are apps that allow you to expand the possibilities for your shooting conditions.

There are hundreds of apps available and more are being developed every day. So this is by no means a full list of iPhone photography apps. They are just some of my favorites … and among the most handy.

*Figure 4-1* *This is the picture as shot.*

# Adobe Photoshop Express

The folks at Adobe created the very versatile Photoshop Express app, which enables you to adjust and edit your images right on your iPhone. With this free app, you can crop an image, adjust exposure and contrast, and even boost the saturation. You can also apply special effects and add borders.

The Photoshop Express app allows you to save your edits as a full-res copy. It also allows you to post your pictures directly to your Facebook, Twitter and **Photoshop.com** accounts.

This app is super easy to use and can give your images a little boost if they need it.

*Figure 4-2* Here's the
same shot with exposure,
contrast and saturation
adjustments made with
the Photoshop Express app
… along with a crop and
a frame.

*Figure 4-3* This is the
same picture with the
Pop effect added for a
Warhol-esque look.

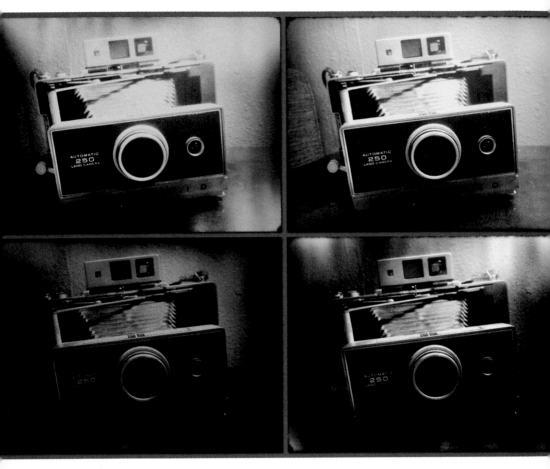

*Figure 4-4* *This shows just a few of the different random effects that are generated by Plastic Bullet.*

# Plastic Bullet

This is currently my favorite photo app. Made to resemble the images from a plastic toy camera, this app goes one step further than all the other similar apps. With Plastic Bullet, each effect that's applied is completely random, so the possibilities are pretty much infinite. Just keep refreshing until you see an effect you like, and then save it. You can save as many different variations of your photograph as you'd like.

This app simulates cross-process film and offers other effects, such as light leaks, black and white, rough edges, lens blur and more. There's not much control over how the effects are applied to your photograph; but, in a sense, that's what photography with a plastic camera is about. It's the unpredictable results that draw people to this kind of camera.

**Figure 4-5** *Plastic Bullet added a vintage flare to my picture of a microphone.*

If you're a Flickr member, you can upload your images straight to your Photostream, and it will automatically post your images into the Plastic Bullet group pool.

This app also allows you to save images at full resolution. For these reasons alone, I think the Plastic Bullet app is well worth the $1.99 it costs.

**Figure 4-6** *This shot was taken at an antique store and processed with LoFi using the EF-2 setting.*

# LoFi

This is a nice free app that simulates the effect of cross-processed film. *Cross processing* is the technique of processing slide film with print film chemicals and vice-versa. Cross processing is also sometimes referred to as *X-pro*. This gives images strange color shifts and high saturation.

LoFi offers twelve different effects and also allows you to place your images into templates that combine two or more photographs into a framed composition.

This app allows you to save at full resolution. The one drawback is that it's relatively slow to process images.

**Figure 4-7** *The LoFi Loca+ setting added a great color to the sky in this shot of the dinosaur in Cabazon, California.*

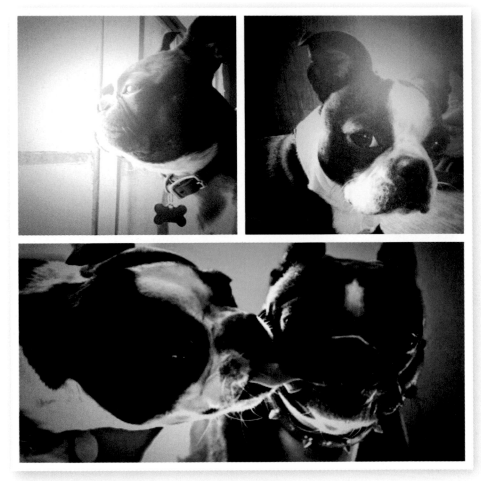

*Figure 4-8* *These three images of my dogs were put together using Diptic.*

# Diptic

Diptic is a very cool app that enables you to make composite images of your iPhone photos using one of nineteen templates. You can put together a photostory, add similar or related photos into one composition, or compile completely different images.

You can either use images from your camera roll or you can take pictures on the spot using the app. Diptic saves files in a medium size.

**Figure 4-9** *Here I used Diptic to put together a musical collage.*

**Figure 4-10** *I used Dash of Color to paint in the signature bright orange Gretsch guitar of the Reverend Horton Heat.*

# Dash of Color

Dash of Color is a free app that turns a selected image to black and white and allows you to "paint" color back in using your finger as a brush on the screen. The brush size can be changed from large (for bigger areas) to a small size (for finer detail).

It's a pretty good app, but I find it difficult to get precise areas painted, because you can't zoom in on the image to really see the details. More often than not, the pictures look sloppy in full size and need to be fixed in Photoshop. For pictures without fine detail though, you can usually get a decent image with this app.

Give it a shot and see what you think. After all, it's free.

*Figure 4-11* *Painting the small details can be kind of tricky.*

*Figure 4-12* *The Sepia effect was applied to this shot of the Texas State Capitol.*

# FilterFX for Free

This is another free app that gives you a choice of nine different filters that you can apply to a selected image. It's a straight-forward no-nonsense app that's quick and easy to use.

**Figure 4-13** *The Vintage filter from Filter FX for Free gave this image a timeless look.*

*Figure 4-14* *The "Sin City" filter applies a very stark black-and-white effect.*

# MovieFX for Free

This is a neat little free app that gives your picture the look of certain movies, such as *Twilight*, *Sin City* and *300*. It also offers generalized effects, such as "horror film" and "security camera."

*Figure 4-15* *Here is a sample of what the MovieFX "Twilight" filter can do.*

# Camera Plus

This is a free camera app that offers more versatility than the standard iPhone camera. It does everything the iPhone camera app does and adds an anti-shake feature, a countdown timer, and a big button feature that allows you to tap anywhere on the screen to take the photo. Keep in mind that this latter option disables the tap-to-focus feature.

You can also crop an image and convert it to black and white within the app.

One of the downfalls to this app is that to add the video capabilities, you need to upgrade for 99¢.

For $1.99 you can upgrade to the Camera Plus Pro app, which offers even more features, including gridlines that can help with composition and filters for both your photos and videos.

*Figure 4-16* *Screenshot of the Camera Plus tools.*

# Gorillacam

| | |
|---|---|
| Self-timer | OFF |
| Time-lapse | OFF |
| Anti-shake | ON |
| Bubble Level | OFF |
| Grid | ON |
| Press Anywhere | OFF |
| 3 Shot Burst | OFF |

Settings    ? More Info

*Figure 4-17  Gorillacam offers lots of options.*

The folks at Joby, maker of the Gorillapod, designed this free app that builds upon the standard camera app and adds a ton of extra features.

Gorillacam has a self-timer that you can set for delay, continuous shooting (by pressing and holding the button) and an instant three-shot burst (with a single tap). It also offers a grid overlay for composing, an anti-shake feature, a bubble level and more.

One of the best things about this app is a time-lapse feature that allows you to take up to 10,000 sequential shots—timed anywhere from one second to two minutes between each shot. Of course you'll need a tripod for this.

The one thing that stops me from using this app as my main camera app is that it doesn't support tap focusing.

# Iron Camera

This is a really cool camera app that allows you to take interesting images with lots of control over the effects. The camera automatically shoots in a square format, and you can choose the resolution size … up to 1600 x 1600 pixels!

My favorite part about this app is the cool retro-futuristic interface. It features levers and dials to change the settings and has a real Industrial vibe to it. Once a photo is taken, you can add film effects and different frames to the image if you wish.

There are a few different versions of this app: the free version, the lite version (which is also free), and the full version that costs 99¢. The free version supports full resolution, and I suggest starting out with this one before upgrading to the paid version, which offers more color effects and frames. The lite version doesn't support high resolution, which limits the image size to 800 x 800 pixels.

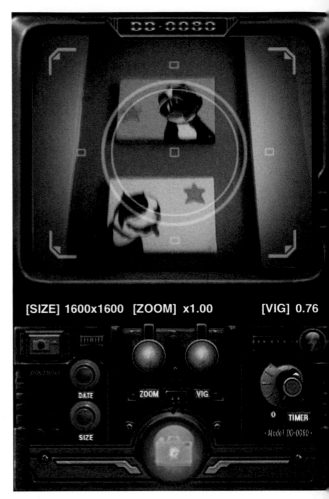

*Figure 4-18* The Iron camera app has an interesting user interface.

**Figure 4-19** *Iron Camera adds a lomo-like effect to this shot from the rotunda of the Texas State Capitol.*

*Figure 4-20* *Hipstamatic lens: Jimmy. Film: Ina's 1969. Flash: Dreampop.*

# Hipstamatic

This is a very popular app that has taken the iPhone camera world by storm. The app re-creates the look of the plastic camera (of the same name) that was invented by two kids from Wisconsin in the eighties. There were only 157 cameras ever made, but they have captured the imagination of lots of iPhone-ographers.

This is a very involved app with lots of different combinations to make your images unique. You can swap out lenses, film types and flash effects to get distinctive images; no two photographs are alike.

The app comes standard with three lenses, three films and two flash effects; but you can buy a number of different "hipstapacks" which include additional lenses, film types and flashes.

**Figure 4-21** *Hipstamatic lens: John S. Film: Pistil. Flash: None.*

Although Hipstamatic is a great app, it does have a few drawbacks. I like the effects, but I don't like that I can't import existing photos from my camera roll into the app to process them. To get the Hipstamatic effect, you must shoot the photograph using the app. And saving takes a bit of time (especially at high-res). So if you want to shoot fast, this really isn't the camera app to use.

Also, the sheer volume of combinations available—of lenses, films and flashes—gets to be overwhelming. It's nice that you can give the camera a shake to randomize the settings.

Back to the upside: The app allows you to upload your images straight to Facebook, Flickr and Tumblr.

**Figure 4-22** *The ClassicTOY app simulates images produced by a plastic toy camera.*

# ClassicTOY – Plastic Toy Camera

This free app simulates—what else?—a plastic toy camera, such as a Holga or Diana. It comes with two different lenses: a standard lens and a double lens, which combines two frames. Additional lenses are available for purchase.

The interface is similar to the Hipstamatic layout and it simulates a camera. The ClassicTOY app comes with 13 different film types that apply different color effects to your pictures.

**Figure 4-23** *This shot was taken using ClassicTOY using the CLS Clear "film."*

*Figure 4-24 moreLomo can make an everyday shot look interesting.*

# moreLomo

This free app simulates photos shot with a Lomo LC-A camera. The Lomo LC-A was an inexpensive camera that was made in Russia and known for severe vignetting (darkening at the image corners), color shifts and soft focus (due to inferior optics). The unpredictable nature of the photographs produced by these cameras caused the images to be unique, which appealed to many young art photographers.

The moreLomo app is very easy to use and has a cool interface that appears as if you are looking through a camera with a dirty viewfinder.

After the photo is taken, a preview appears. You can switch between the original image and the Lomo version for comparison.

**Figure 4-25**  *moreLomo images are unpredictable and unique, like this surrealistic bear shot.*

*Figure 4-26* *The moreMono (Red Edition) is a great app to quickly get a selective color image.*

## moreMono (Red Edition)

This is another freebie from the same company that produced moreLomo. It's a pretty simple app that operates the same as the standard iPhone camera.

After a picture is taken, the app de-saturates all colors except for the ones with reddish hues. It has three different settings: Portrait, Normal and Maximum. The effect is applied automatically, so you don't have to paint in the color as you do in other apps.

You can also import pictures from your photo library or camera roll to be edited with this app.

**Figure 4-27** *Using moreMono added an interesting effect to this shot of the Caldwell County Courthouse in Lockhart, Texas.*

*Figure 4-28* Helga from Camera Bag produces the look of images shot with a Holga camera.

# Camera Bag

This is one of the first camera apps that I bought when I got my first iPhone, and it was one of my favorites for awhile. I've since discovered new apps that do certain effects better, but Camera Bag does a very good job. And it offers a lot of different effects, including a Holga and Lomo effect (called Helga and Lolo), a Polaroid (which reproduces the color quite accurately, I might add), some vintage stylings with borders … and more.

I highly recommend this app if you're not into buying a lot of apps and want to get the most bang for your buck.

*Figure 4-29*  *Instant from Camera Bag simulates the distinctive Polaroid look.*

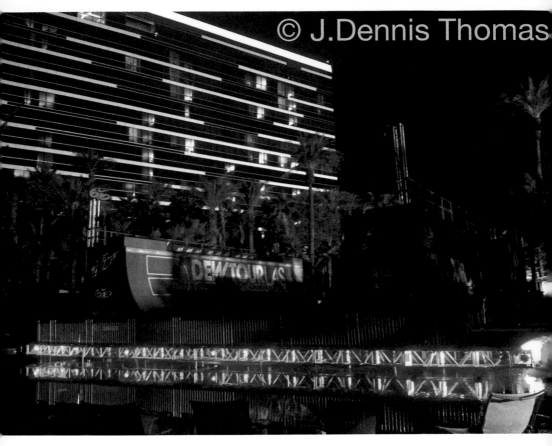

*Figure 4-30  Add a water mark to a photo using the Impression app.*

## Impression

The Impression app allows you to place a watermark on any photo in your library. You can use this to add copyright information or to quickly add text to a photo.

# RetroCamera

This app has two versions—a free one and a paid one. The free one imprints the app developer's name on your images.

RetroCamera isn't a very quick or easy app to use, but it does have some cool features. It's got more than a dozen types of film simulations and a bunch of great frames, film edges and textures.

The one huge drawback to this app is that it saves pictures at a very low resolution. The only thing you can really do with the pictures is view them on the iPhone. In fact, the resolution is so low that images are barely viewable on a computer, and they're almost not even reproducible in print.

If the app is updated to save full resolution files, then it will be great for adding cool effects to your iPhone pictures. Until then, I suggest that you save your money and use the free version.

**Figure 4-31** *This is a composite of three images processed with RetroCamera.*

*Figure 4-32* *The photo starts out undeveloped.*

# ShakeItPhoto

ShakeItPhoto is a Polaroid simulator that allows you to experience the full joy of using an instant camera. Take the picture, and you can hear and see the photo slide out. Watch the picture develop right before your eyes. Yep, you can even shake the iPhone to help it develop faster!

**Figure 4-33** *Shake it and watch your photograph develop into the finished product.*

**Figure 4-34** *This Infinicam setting (code YX1-XAT7) added the perfect look to this shot of vintage motorcycles.*

# Infinicam

This relatively new app was designed by the same folks who created Camera Bag. The best way I can describe this app is as a cross between Plastic Bullet and Hipstamatic. Take the randomness of Plastic Bullet and the cool frames from Hipstamatic, and you get Infinicam.

Each time you tap the New Camera button, Infinicam generates a random selection of colors, effects and borders. If you find a combination that you really like, you can add it as a favorite and use it again and again.

**Figure 4-35** *Among the numerous film edges available in this app, this is one of my favorites (code Q5E-2368).*

You can also e-mail the photos you take with this app straight to your friends. Your e-mail will include a link that allows your Infinicam-using friends to quickly access the same effect. Each effect has a numbered code that can be entered manually, so that's a second way you can share settings.

Infinicam offers a slew of film-type borders—from slides to 35mm film edges and more. The app also allows you to crop the original image from inside the app *before* applying an effect. So you can fix any composition issues quickly and easily.

*Figure 4-36* *Darkroom can help you get more usable images when taking pictures in dark areas.*

# Darkroom

Darkroom is a free app that uses the iPhone's accelerometer to detect movement. It waits until the iPhone is still before snapping a shot. This allows you to get relatively sharp pictures in subdued light. Of course this won't help with fast-moving subjects, due to the longer shutter speeds required when the light is low; but for relatively static scenes, this app works great to keep your low-light pictures clear.

***Figure 4-37***  *Without Darkroom, this shot might have been a blurry mess!*

*Figure 4-38* *I used the FudgeCam effect to snap this shot of the creature from the black lagoon.*

# Retro Camera

Not to be confused with the RetroCamera (all one word) that was covered earlier, this Retro Camera is another funky little app that replicates toy cameras and old film. It's got a cool interface and a selection of five different camera effects.

The effects aren't really *great*, and some are better than others, but it is a free app. The FudgeCan and Little Orange Box are the best. Xolaroid totally misses the mark.

It's very easy to use and saves images to the Camera Roll fairly quickly. The main downside is that Retro Camera Plus saves images in a fairly low resolution, even though you have an option to save as a high-resolution image in the settings.

**Figure 4-39** *The Little Orange Box effect adds some texture and a cool faded-out border.*

*Figure 4-40* *The Cross Process app adds funky colors and a retro vibe to this shot.*

# Cross Process

This inexpensive app re-creates the effect of film that has been *cross-processed*. This is a technique in which slide film is developed in chemicals for print film and vice-versa. The final outcome of this technique is odd color shifts and high contrast.

One interesting thing about the Cross Process app is that you can watch the photo "develop" … similar to the ShakeItPhoto app, which was designed by the same folks.

You can control the colors somewhat by turning the color filters on and off. And I discovered that if all the filters are turned off, you get a negative-like effect, which is very interesting.

**Figure 4-41**  *Cross Process makes the colors in this image really vibrant.*

***Figure 4-42*** *I used PanoLab to stitch together four shots to make this panoramic shot of White Sands, New Mexico.*

# PanoLab

PanoLab is a great tool for the landscape iPhone photographers out there. This app allows you to link up to thirty images and stitch them together to create magnificent panoramas. You can also adjust the exposure and white balance, so that your photos match perfectly. This gives you a seamless super-wide panoramic view.

The only downside is that it can be difficult to line up images exactly because of the small size of the screen. Otherwise this is a pretty good app.

Keep in mind that your images will need to be cropped to get clean edges.

## Chapter 5

# Create iPhone Video

Shooting video with your iPhone is similar to shooting photographs. Just about all the photography principles covered in Chapters 2 and 3 apply to video as well.

However, since video isn't static like a photograph, there are additional issues to consider when shooting … especially if you have an audience to consider. Movement and sound are very important elements of video, so special attention must be paid to these facets.

As with photographs, the iPhone's ability to shoot video allows you to capture special moments and to share them right away.

*Figure 5-1* *Remember the Rule of Thirds … even when shooting video.*

# Composition

As I mentioned on the previous page, most of the rules of photo composition apply to video as well. The Rule of Thirds, focus and backgrounds are three particularly important aspects of composition. And by composing your videos well, you make them appear more professional and easier to watch. That's good for everyone, right?

*Figure 5-2* *The Gary Fong tripod adapter allowed me to effortlessly pan along with this racecar.*

# Keep It Sure and Steady

One of the worst things you can do to your viewers is make them watch jittery, shaky videos. As I mentioned in Chapter 2, keeping your elbows squeezed in to your sides will help you keep your hands steadier (and avoid camera shake) than when you shoot at arm's length. Leaning against something stable like a wall can also help.

There are a number of manufacturers that make tripods and other devices that can help you keep your iPhone steady. The Joby Gorillamobile is a good one.

Right along with shaky video, footage that features frequent changes in zooming can be annoying for viewers, too. Not only does zooming in and out a lot make your video even more jittery than camera shake alone, it can make it difficult for a viewer to see your images.

Another reason to avoid zooming is, as I said before, the iPhone uses a digital zoom that markedly degrades the image quality of the video. If you must zoom, I recommend using *sneaker zoom*, which translates into getting physically closer to your subject.

*Figure 5-3*  *Fast side-to-side movements can cause distortion in your photos and video.*

# Panning

*Panning* is the sweeping—usually side-to side—movement a camera makes. In still photography, panning is used to track along with a subject; in videography, a pan shot can be used to follow the subject, to move back and forth between two subjects, or to simply show a whole scene by sweeping across it.

Panning with the iPhone is best done in a slow, fluid movement. Moving too fast introduces *skew* which causes the video to look like it's warped. This can also be observed in still photos. Panning back and forth quickly (whip pans) can introduce a Jell-O-like effect.

*Figure 5-4* *The iPhone's tap to focus feature ensures that right subject is featured in your images.*

## Tap to Focus

Keep your subject in focus. With the 3Gs and 4G iPhone models, you can tap an area to selectively focus. You can use the tap focus feature to shift focus from a subject in the foreground to a subject in the background or vice-versa.

*Figure 5-5*  *Leave some headroom.*

# Framing Heads

When shooting videos of people, especially close-ups of faces, there are a few different things to keep in mind. First, you want to be sure that you leave enough room under the chin so that it stays in frame when your subject is talking. But you also want to leave a little room at the top of the head as well.

When a person's head is at three-quarter or profile view, be sure to keep some room in front of the eyes. Your subject should never be looking directly at the edge of the frame.

**Figure 5-6** *The telephone pole is causing a merger here.*
*Changing the angle slightly left or right will eliminate this.*

# Mergers

Another thing to look for when shooting photos or video of people are *mergers*. Mergers occur when your subject overlaps background objects, which appear to be growing out of your subject. When shooting, take a close look at the background in relation to your subject before you tap the record button.

*Figure 5-7  Unusual perspectives can make video footage more interesting.*

# Perspective

Try to find an interesting perspective for your videos. Shooting at eye-level is usually the most obvious choice, but this can be unimaginative.

Try shooting from far above or far below your subject to add some interest to your shots. Shoot multiple angles of the same subject and link them together using the iMovie app to create a much more dynamic video. The iMovie app is covered in Chapter 5.

Try using floor-level shots for your pets and kids.

*Figure 5-8* *Keep an eye out for interesting locations to shoot your videos.*

# Plan your Shots

To make the most interesting videos, take the time to plan out your shots. Think like a filmmaker.

Even if you're just shooting a child's birthday party, scope out the scene ahead of time and find the best angles from which to shoot. This will make your iPhone-shot home video look much more professional.

Use the iPhone Notes app to write down a few these tips and refer to them when setting up your shots.

*Figure 5-9* *Tell a story with your video footage.*

# Shoot Sequences

Instead of creating one wide continuous shot that follows the action of your subject, consider making sequence shots … and then edit them together to tell a story.

For example, instead of a wide shot of a golfer teeing off, you could make this more compelling by shooting a series of small vignettes.

First, show a close-up of the golf bag. Next, get a wide shot of the golfer selecting a driver and a close-up of the golfer placing the ball on the tee. Then cut away to a wide shot of the swing. Get a long shot of the ball flying down the fairway, and end with a shot of the ball landing on the green.

*Figure 5-10* *Remember that if the sound in your video is too loud, it can be distorted.*

## The Impact of Sound

Keep in mind that the microphone for iPhone video is on the iPhone, so the closer you are to your subject the better the sound quality will be.

Also be aware of background noise. The microphone picks up all sounds; so in a noisy environment, background noise may drown out your subject.

***Figure 5-11*** *Front lighting keeps the details sharp.*

# Front Lighting

The best type of lighting for shooting video is front lighting. Using it will ensure that you get good detail in your scene. Remember to keep the sun at your back for best results.

*Figure 5-12*  *Backlighting can be disastrous for a video.*

# Watch for Backlighting

When shooting still pictures, backlighting can have an interesting effect. But when shooting video, it's almost always a bad idea.

Backlighting leaves the subject in a shadow, which can cause problems, especially when shooting video of people. You won't be able to see expressions on their face in this lighting setup.

If you have an iPhone 4 and you're in a situation where you have no choice but to use backlighting, switch on the flash LED light to fill in the shadows. I recommend this only as a last option.

**Figure 5-13** *Trimming a video from the Camera Roll is quick and easy.*

# Trimming

The iPhone allows you to do some rudimentary video editing right in the camera for short clips. You can trim the beginning and end of a video to create more concise clips.

To trim a video, select the video file from the Camera Roll. At the top of the video, you'll see a timeline of the video with small clips. Drag the sliders from the beginning and end and move them inward to shorten the video.

You can preview the edit by tapping "Play." When you're satisfied with your edit, tap the Trim button. This accesses up a pop-up menu that offers a couple of options (described below):

**Trim Original** overwrites the original clip and saves the trimmed version only.

**Save as New Clip** preserves the original video and saves the trimmed version as a copy, preserving the original video clip.

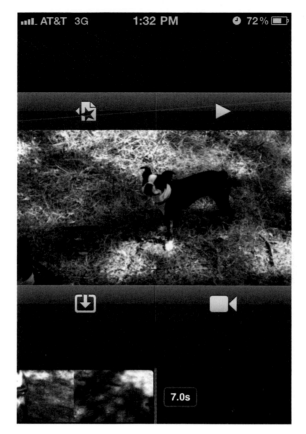

*Figure 5-14* *Use the iPhone iMovie app for easy video editing.*

# iMovie app

Apple has released a rudimentary video-editing app based upon their iMovie video editing software that is included with all Mac computers.

It's a pretty simple app that allows you to drag already recorded clips into a timeline, or you can directly record video into the timeline.

There are a few different Themes available: Modern, Bright, Travel, Playful and News. You can insert titles to these themes, and each theme has music that can be turned on or off.

This app is great for linking a few clips together on the fly to post to YouTube or to email to friends and family. Note that YouTube is covered in Chapter 8.

# Chapter 6

## Edit with Photoshop Elements 9

Although Adobe has an iPhone app for editing your photos on the device (Photoshop Express), it's very limited in functionality. So if you're serious about your iPhone pictures and you want to make them look the best you can, check into getting Photoshop Elements (PSE) for editing your images on your computer.

This inexpensive software is Adobe's simpler version of its photo-editing powerhouse program: Photoshop. Photoshop Elements is available for both Mac and PC.

Although Photoshop Elements is fairly simple, it is still an incredibly powerful tool and enables you to do all types of editing, color correction, cropping and more.

This program has many different editing tools, and there are lots of different techniques you can learn. To help get you started, this chapter covers the most basic adjustments and edits. Find instructions for transferring image files from your iPhone to your computer in Chapter 8.

*Tip: You can download a free 30-day trial of Photoshop Elements 9 at Adobe.com.*

# Quick Fix Mode

The Quick Fix Mode is meant to make editing your photos as simple as possible. Quick Fix presents you with a limited amount of tools, and all of the necessary adjustments are organized in easy-to-use tabs with sliders.

To begin exploring here, click on "Auto" to let PSE do the adjustments for you. Then, you can use the sliders to adjust the settings to your taste.

There are five tabs that appear on the right side of the image preview:

**Smart Fix** does an overall adjustment and evens out shadows and highlights.

The **Lighting** option allows you to fine-tune the tonality in the Shadows, Mid-tones and Highlights … separately. You can brighten the shadows, darken the highlights, and either darken or brighten the mid-tones.

**Color** makes it possible to boost the saturation for more vibrant colors, or to decrease it for subdued tones. Using the Hue slider, you can change the colors of the image in relation to each other. For example, if you change the hue of the yellows to blue, then the blues will turn yellow.

The **Balance** slider allows you to make adjustments to the white balance.

**Sharpness** refers to the crispness of focus in an image. When you're finished with editing a photograph, you may want to sharpen it a bit. Be sure not to overdo though. A little bit of sharpening goes a long way. Over-sharpening can cause an image to appear grainy.

**Figure 6-1** *PSE 9 Quick Fix Mode makes it easy to enhance your iPhone images.*

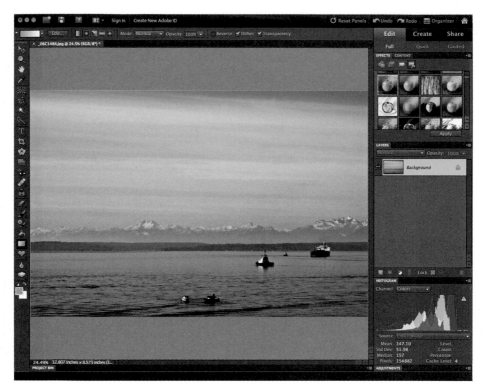

**Figure 6-2** *Editing your iPhone photos using the Full Edit menu offers a lot more options for creative expression.*

# Full Edit Mode

This mode allows you a lot more flexibility in editing an image. Full Edit Mode offers 21 tools within the toolbar on the left side of the window. The functionality of some of these tools is covered in this chapter.

You can also do non-destructive editing by using adjustment layers, applying filters and more. In the next few sections, we'll cover the tools you'll need to do most of your basic image editing.

Aspect Ratio

Crop Tool

*Figure 6-3* *The PSE 9 Crop tool can eliminate edge space from an image to better emphasize details in a photograph.*

Confirm ⎯⎤  ⎡⎯ Cancel

# Cropping

The Crop tool is the ninth tool from the top in the Tool bar. You can click on it, or you can access it more quickly by pressing C—the keyboard shortcut.

Once the Crop tool is selected, you simply mouse the tool over the image and then click and drag until you have recomposed the image by removing some of the edge.

If you need to crop to a specific aspect ratio for printing, click on the Aspect Ratio tab in the upper left corner. A drop-down menu appears with options for different sizes. Click on the size that best fits your need. If you have a custom size in mind, you can set the dimensions in the Width and Height boxes.

When you are satisfied with the crop selection, simply press "Enter" or click on the Confirm button, which appears as a green checkmark at the bottom right of your crop selection.

To exit without cropping, press "Escape" or the Cancel button (located next the Confirm button).

Canvas Options

Straighten Tool

*Figure 6-4 The PSE 9 Straighten tool helps you align the image.*

# Straighten Tool

The Straighten tool is the twelfth icon from the top in the Tool bar. The keyboard shortcut for the Straighten tool is P. This tool is used to realign an image to make sure that the horizon or a vertical element in the image is straight.

After selecting the Straighten tool, click on the Canvas Options tab at the top left of the window. Select "Crop to Remove Background" from the drop-down menu. This allows PSE to automatically crop the image rather than simply rotating the canvas.

Mouse the cursor to one side of the plane that you want to be straight. In the case of this landscape image, it's the left side of the horizon. Click and drag the cursor to the other side of the straight plane. Releasing the drag automatically straightens the image.

If you aren't satisfied with the results, you can undo by pressing CMD+Z on Macs or ALT+Z on PCs. (This "undo" technique applies to all changes you make in PSE.)

*Figure 6-5*  *Click on the layer mask before you paint on it.*

# Adjustment Layers

One of the reasons people choose Photoshop Elements over other editing software (such as iPhoto) is that PSE enables users to make adjustments in layers, which don't affect the original image.

A layer in Photoshop Elements is like a sheet of cellophane that's placed over the original image. Any changes you want to make are done to the cellophane. So if you don't like what you see, simply peel it off and start again.

Use the Brush tool (B) to paint on an adjustment layer mask and reveal what's underneath.

# Levels

The Levels adjustment is one of the most powerful tools you have in PSE. You can use this one adjustment layer to make both tonal and color adjustments.

There are two ways to adjust the Levels. The first is to type CMD+L (or ALT+L for PC). This brings up the Levels dialog box and allows you to adjust the levels directly on the image pixels.

The second method, the one I recommend using, is to create a Levels adjustment layer. Do this by clicking on the Adjustment Layers button on the Layers tab on the right side of the window. Select "Levels" from the drop-down menu to create a Levels layer.

Using an adjustment layer allows you make your edits without affecting the underlying pixels of the original image. You can turn the layer on and off by clicking the Eyeball button on the layer. You can also go back in and make additional adjustments to the levels at any time.

Once your Levels adjustment layer has been created, you'll notice that the Adjustment tab appears underneath the Layers tab. In the Adjustment tab, you'll see the Levels dialog box.

The Levels adjustment is the quickest and easiest way to make the two most important tweaks to your images: tonal adjustments and color correction. It only takes a few seconds, but this tool gives you so much control. I recommend playing around with a few images to get the hang of how to use Levels.

*Figure 6-6* *The PSE 9 Levels tool allows you to adjust the levels directly on the image pixels.*

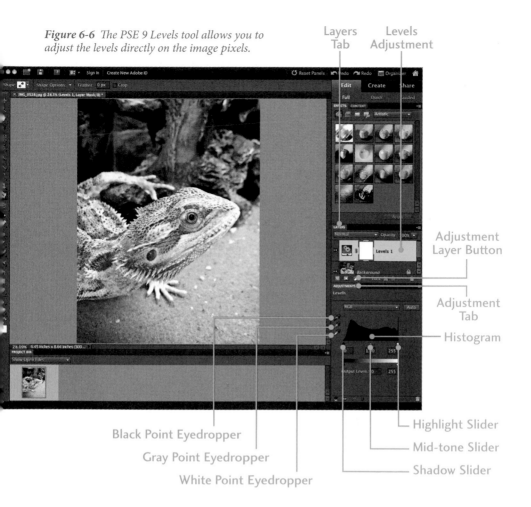

Layers
Tab

Levels
Adjustment

Adjustment
Layer Button

Adjustment
Tab

Histogram

Black Point Eyedropper

Gray Point Eyedropper

White Point Eyedropper

Highlight Slider

Mid-tone Slider

Shadow Slider

# Histogram

The Levels dialog box shows a *histogram*, which is a graph that represents the lightness (or luminosity) values of all the pixels in the image. The graph shows the darkest to lightest values, ranging from a value of 0 (absolute black) to 255 (absolute white).

Notice the three triangle sliders located under the histogram. The black one on the left (shadow slider) makes the image darker, and the white one (highlight slider) on the right makes the image lighter. Moving these two sliders toward each other increases the contrast in your image. The grey middle slider (mid-tone slider) allows you to adjust the overall brightness of the image.

The first thing to do is look at the histogram. The graph should stretch evenly from one end to the other, like the example in figure 6.7. If you have a gap on either side, move the slider over to where the histogram starts. This will give you a good starting point. Next, move the middle slider back and forth until the image looks good to you. Voilá! That's it for the tonal adjustments.

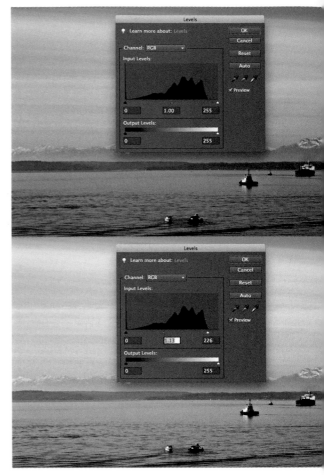

***Figure 6-7*** *Moving the white point into where the graph starts brought out the whites in the image and increased the contrast.*

**Figure 6-8** *Click on a neutral grey area, such as indicated by the green square, to color correct using Levels.*

# Color Correction Using Levels

Next up is color correction. See the three eyedroppers in the Levels dialog box in the Adjustments tab? The black eyedropper is the black point; the grey eyedropper is the grey point; and the white one is the white point. They're color-coded for easy identification.

The quickest and easiest way to do color correction is to click on the grey point eyedropper and click on an area in the image that should be neutral grey (or close to it). This will adjust the color of the whole image. This is a useful method for correcting for white balance errors, too.

# Hue and Saturation

As with the Levels adjustment, there are two ways that the Hue and Saturation adjustments can be accomplished. You can type CMD+U (Alt+U for PC) to make the adjustments directly to the image pixels. But my preferred way is to create an adjustment layer by clicking on the Adjustment Layer button and selecting "Hue and Saturation" from the drop-down menu. The Hue and Saturation dialog box is displayed in the Adjustment tab.

Adjusting the hue changes the colors, and changing saturation adjusts the purity of the colors. By default, when moving the Hue slider, all of the colors are changed. But you can adjust specific ranges of colors by clicking on the color range drop-down menu and selecting a color range (reds, yellows, greens, etc).

When adjusting hue in an image, you want to be pretty careful. Even minor movements of the hue slider make a tremendous impact.

The Saturation slider allows you to make colors more vibrant in your photograph … or more muted. Slide right to enhance vibrancy; slide left to mute colors. Generally, I like to bump the saturation to about +20 to make an image really pop.

By pulling the Saturation slider all the way to the left, you can remove all the color from your image and convert it to black and white.

By clicking on the Colorize box, you can turn your image monochrome and use the Hue slider to select a color … as I did in figure 6.10.

The lightness slider adds white or black to the colors in the image. Personally, I don't touch this slider, because it takes the contrast right out of the image.

*Figure 6-9* *PSE 9 Hue and Saturation adjustments can overhaul the look and feel of your images.*

Add New Layer Button

Hue/Saturation Adjustment Layer

Adjustment Layer Button

Color Range Drop Down Menu

Lightness Slider

Hue Slider   Saturation Slider   Colorize Box

*Figure 6-10* *Add a color tint to a monochrome image to make a boring photograph more interesting.*

# Retouching

One of the best features of Photoshop Elements is its ability to retouch blemishes quickly and easily using the Healing Brush tool. To access this tool, click on the Healing Brush tool button. It's the fourteenth icon down from the top. Or simply use the keyboard shortcut (J).

Select a brush size at the top left side of the window. The brush size should be just a little larger than the spot you are retouching. You can use the left and right bracket keys on the keyboard to make the brush larger or smaller.

Position the Healing Brush tool over the blemish you wish to remove ... and click.

The tool is *content aware*, which means that it takes image information from the surrounding pixels and uses it to fill in the pixels of the spot you are retouching with pixels of a similar color. I have to say, it works very well as long as you stay away from areas with abrupt contrast changes.

You can use this tool right on the original image layer, but ... as always ... I recommend using a layer. This way you can reverse any changes and you can turn the layer on and off for comparison. Simply click the Add New Layer button at the bottom left of the Layers tab to get started.

**Figure 6-11** *The iron bar in this photo is distracting.*

**Figure 6-12** *I used the Retouch tool to get rid of the distracting element.*

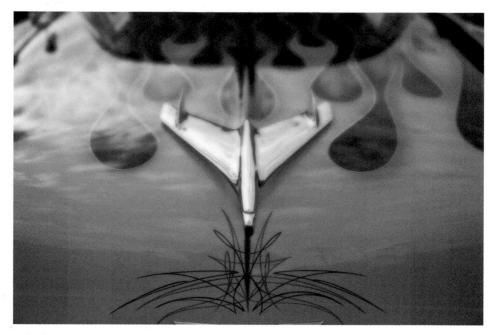

**Figure 6-13** *Using layers, masks, a blur filter and the gradient tool, I faked a shallow depth of field in this image.*

# Simulating Shallow Depth of Field

Since it's very difficult to achieve a shallow depth of field with the iPhone camera, I've developed a simple way to fake it very easily using a blur effect and the Gradient tool. Check it out:

1. Open the file in PSE.

2. Make a copy layer by dragging the Background layer down to the Layer button.

3. Click on Filter > Blur > Gaussian blur. This brings up a dialog box. Set the blur radius to 25 pixels.

4. Click on the Layer Mask button to add a layer mask to the top layer. The Layer Mask button is located next to the Layer button.

5. Select the Gradient tool. You can click on it in the Tool bar or press G.

6. Place the cursor at the bottom of the image and drag up to the top. This will leave the bottom of the image sharp and gradually fade out to a blur, simulating a shallow depth of field.

**Note:** This technique doesn't work well with all images. It works best with images that are more or less on a flat plane. Experiment with the different blurs and images to see what works best for your photographs.

*Figure 7-1* iPhoto automatically sorts your images into folders by date.

## Chapter 7

# Edit with iPhoto

Apple's iPhoto software is a powerful editing and photo management application. It is only available for the Mac.

iPhoto allows you to import photos to your computer straight from the iPhone, so you can organize, view and edit them all in one program.

Keep in mind that the tips in this chapter apply not only to your iPhone photos, but to all your digital photos. You can use these tips on photos taken with a compact camera or a DSLR as easily as you can use them to enhance your iPhone images.

# Edit in Full Screen

When using iPhoto to edit your images, the best way to start is by entering Full Screen. This gets rid of any extraneous elements and displays the image on a black background, so you can focus on editing without any distracting folders or tabs. Enter Full Screen mode by clicking on the button at the bottom left of the screen or by using the Mac keyboard shortcut (cmd+opt+F).

Select a photo by clicking on it, and then enter Full Screen mode. To start editing, click on the Edit button, which is located at the bottom right ... nested among four other buttons. The Edit button appears as a pencil icon.

Once the Edit button is clicked, a menu palette will pop up on the right side of the screen. This palette has three tabs: Quick Fixes, Effects and Adjust.

Quick Fixes    Effects    Adjust

**Figure 7-2** *Navigation tabs can be found in the upper right corner when working in Full Screen mode.*

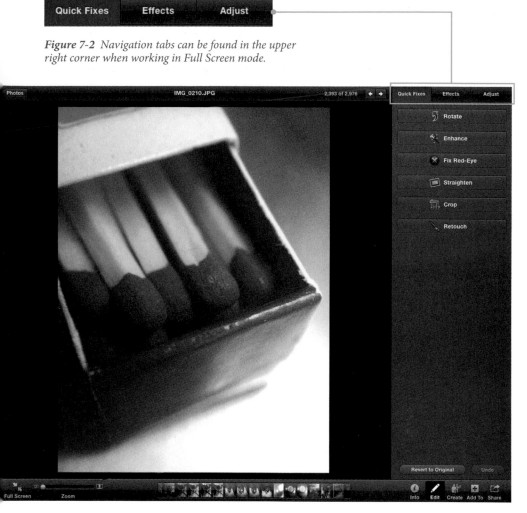

**Figure 7-3** *Take a look at the Quick Fixes menu.*

# The Quick Fixes Tab

Quick Fixes allows you to make some minor, basic adjustments to your image quickly and without much effort. This is where you do your cropping, rotating, retouching and more. There are six options here:

Use the **Rotate** option to reorient your photo from landscape to portrait (or vice versa). Click the button once to rotate the photo 90° counter-clockwise. Click once more to rotate 180°.

**Enhance** is a Quick Fixes button that automatically adds a little color boost to the photo to make it pop.

The **Fix Red-Eye** feature should be self-explanatory. It fixes red-eye, which is caused by a firing flash. When you click on the button, a drop-down menu appears. Use the slider to adjust the brush size to match the pupil of the offending eye. Place the brush over the eye and click. Press the Done button when the red-eye is gone.

**Straighten** is used to correct crooked images, such as a landscape with a horizon that isn't quite level. Use the angle slider to adjust ±10°. A grid is available to help with lining up things.

**Crop** enables you to recompose images. Use this tool to remove elements you don't want to be seen or to tighten your image's composition.

**Retouch** is one of the greatest tools available for digital photography. The retouch tool magically fixes almost any spot on an image—be it a blemish on a face or speck of dirt on a white shirt. Use the Size slider to set the brush size. You want the brush to be just a bit larger than the spot to be retouched. Click to select. It's just that easy. This tool works best on areas without a lot of contrast. Be careful when using this near areas with abrupt color or contrast change.

**Figure 7-4** *The Quick Fixes tab offers six different photo-editing tools.*

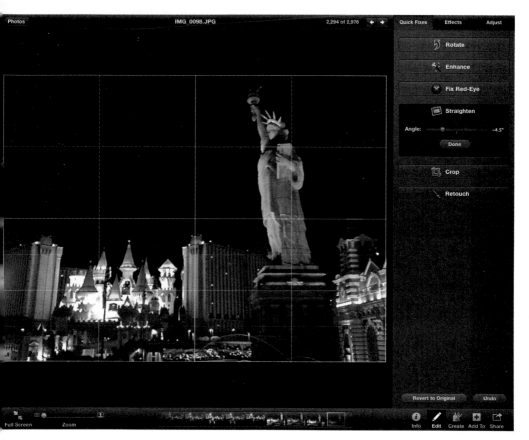

**Figure 7-5** *Use the Straighten tool to fix photos with crooked horizons.*

# The Effects Tab

The Effects tab allows you to quickly make broad changes to color and contrast and to create a few edge effects. Among the 15 options it offers, most can be combined. The exceptions are Lighten and Darken … and Warmer and Cooler, which work opposite of each other and thus cancel out the other.

See the next few sections for details on how to use this tab to make tonality and color adjustments and photo effects.

**Figure 7-6** *The Effects tab is the second of three main sections shown in the Full Screen mode.*

**Figure 7-7** *The Effects menu contains 15 different options.*

# Tonality and Color Adjustments

This section of controls is available in the Effects tab. These tools allow you to make adjustments in tonality by lightening, darkening, and increasing contrast in your image. You can also add photo filter color effects here, like warming and cooling the image and boosting the saturation.

Click on the buttons multiple times to add more of the effect. Once the effect is maxed out, you'll notice that the button grays out.

**Lighten** brightens the luminosity of the image, bringing the highlights up to pure white and brightening the mid-tones and shadow areas.

Use **Darken** to deepen the shade of the photo's overall tone. This tool mutes the highlights and flattens the mid-tones and shadows … without actually bringing them to pure black (as long as the image is properly exposed).

**Contrast** emphasizes the overall difference between lights and darks in an image. It can add definition to a flat image. This option is relatively subtle in its effect.

**Warmer** adds an overall orange color to the tone of the image, which gives it a nice warm glow that's similar to an evening sunset.

Conversely, the **Cooler** option adds a blue tint to the image to make it look … well, cooler.

Clicking on **Saturate** increases the vividness of colors in the image.

*Figure 7-8* Tonality and color adjustment
tools are available in the Effects tab.

*Figure 7-9* I used the Effects tab to make this image warmer and to add contrast.

# Photo Effects

This section of the Effects tab simulates some of the visual impressions that photographers created in the traditional darkroom.

The **B&W** option converts the image to black and white—plain and simple. This can make your image stark and ethereal and add a little more interest to what may otherwise be a bland image. Sometimes taking away color actually adds to an image.

**Sepia** is another simple one-click effect. The Sepia button converts an image to sepia tone, which gives a picture the look of a vintage photograph. It's a warmer version of black and white.

**Antique** gives the highlights in your image a warm tone while adding a cool greenish tone to the shadows. You can add a little of this effect or a lot by choosing the strength on a scale of one through nine.

**Matte** adds at a white oval border around the edges of the picture. You can set the effect strength anywhere from 1 to 25 … with 25 leaving only a tiny spot of the picture visible.

Similar to Matte, the **Vignette** option adds a black oval border around the edge of the image.

**Edge Blur** is a very cool effect that gives a subtle blurring effect that radiates in from the edges. Edge Blur can add a shallow depth of field effect to your iPhone photos, which usually have a relatively deep depth of field. You can set the intensity of this effect from one to eleven. This effect works particularly well with high contrast images and can give your images a dreamy feeling.

Simply enough, **Fade** reduces saturation … or fades out the colors. The settings go from one to nine, with one being very slight and nine appearing almost as a black and white image with a distinct bluish tint.

**Boost** increases both saturation and contrast proportionally.

Use **None** to change all the settings back to zero. You can also use the Revert to Original button to do this.

Figure 7-10  *Access nine different photo effects in the iPhoto Effects tab.*

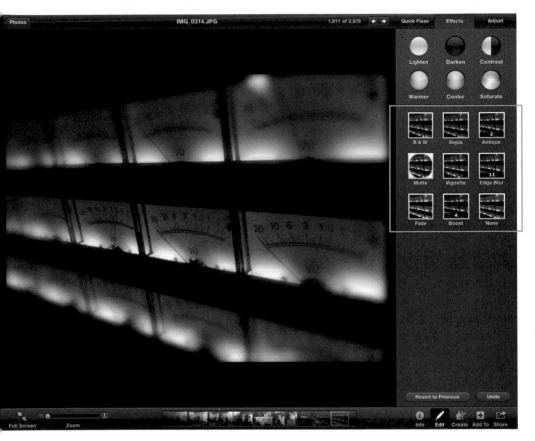

Figure 7-11  *This image was adjusted using the Antique, Edge Blur and Boost effects.*

# The Adjust Tab

The Adjust tab is a little more advanced than the Quick Fixes or Effects tabs, but it offers much more control and allows you to address the changes to images in finer detail. This is key to getting your photographs to look exactly as you envisioned them.

Although the controls here are a little more advanced, don't let that dissuade you from using them. They are very easy to use once you have a little understanding of what they do. You'll get the hang of it in no time after reading this section.

Over the next few pages, we'll cover some of these controls, including Levels, tools for adjusting Tonality and Details, and White Balance.

**Figure 7-12** *The Adjust tab is the third tab available in the Full Screen mode.*

**Figure 7-13** *The Adjust menu offers options that give you much more control over your image edits.*

# Levels

This is probably the most important tool in iPhoto for making tonal adjustments. It's much more subtle than using the Auto or Quick Fixes settings, but you can make sure that your image has the perfect exposure by using the *histogram*—a graph that represents the lightness (or luminosity) values of all the pixels in the image. The histogram shows areas in your image from darkest to lightest, ranging from a value of 0% (absolute black) to 100% (absolute white).

Three triangle sliders are located under the histogram. The one at the left (black point slider) makes the image darker, and the one at the right (white point slider) makes the image lighter. Sliding the two toward each other increases the contrast in your image.

The middle slider (mid-tone slider) allows you to adjust the overall brightness of the image.

The histogram should stretch evenly from one end of the screen to the other, like the example in figure 7.15. If you have a gap on either side, move the slider to where the histogram starts. This will give you a good starting point. Next, move the middle slider back and forth until the image looks good to you.

**Figure 7-14**  *Find a histogram in the Adjust tab.*

**Figure 7-15**  *This figure was a little overexposed, so I dragged the black point slider up 10%. This darkened the shadow areas and gave the image more contrast.*

# Adjusting Tonality

This section allows you to do more broad adjustments to an image's tonality than Levels. You can also increase the vividness of colors in this section of the Adjust tab tools.

If your picture has a good exposure and you did some tweaking in Levels, you shouldn't need to touch the **Exposure** slider at all. But if your image is noticeably over- or underexposed, this is where you should start. Keep in mind that this is not a cure-all; but it will help. Slide it to the right to add exposure (lighten) and to the left to take away exposure (darken).

**Contrast** makes the darks darker and the lights lighter, so the gap between them grows. Again, if you've set your Levels properly, you may not need this slider at all.

The **Saturation** slider controls the purity of the colors and can make your pictures more or less vivid. Sliding to the right makes the colors more vivid and sliding to the left mutes the colors. Pushing the slider all the way left takes away all color, leaving you with black and white image.

A great feature of the Saturation slider is the "Avoid saturating skin tones" click box. This allows you to saturate all colors, but it leaves the oranges and yellows that are close to the color of skin relatively untouched for a more natural look.

**Figure 7-16**  *Access sliders to adjust exposure, contrast and saturation in the Adjust tab.*

**Figure 7-17**  *I increased the Contrast and Saturation on this photo to make the colors "pop."*

# Adjust the Details

This section of the Adjust tab allows you to change some of the minor details and fine-tune your image. The available tools in this section are described below.

**Definition** is a useful slider. It adds some subtle separation between the shadows and the mid-tones to make the subject stand out just a bit more. It's especially great for bringing out the detail in a subject with texture. Be careful when using on portraits; it can bring out unflattering details of the skin.

The **Highlights** slider helps add detail in highlight areas that have minor overexposure.

Conversely, using the **Shadows** slider allows you to bring out some detail from the shadow area of an image.

**Sharpness** adds a bit of definition to your image on a pixel-to-pixel level. This gives the picture the appearance of being sharper. Use Sharpening with a light hand though, because sharpening increases the noise detail as well as the image detail. Adding sharpness in editing doesn't make up for an out-of-focus image.

Use the **De-noise** option to reduce the noise artifacts in your image that are caused by shooting in low-light situations. This is another tool that requires a *very* light hand. No question, Apple needs to do some refining work on this tool. Any setting above 15 causes your image to appear smeared and almost paint-like. I prefer to have a little noise than a smeary image.

**Figure 7-18** *The Adjust tab offers five sliders that help you fine-tune your image.*

**Figure 7-19** *On this image, I boosted the Definition to bring out the detail in the bricks.*

# White Balance

This is the section to use for making adjustments to the white balance settings and achieving a natural color in your photo. The tools described below are easy-to-use and make a big difference to the look of your images.

Use the **Temperature** option to fix problems with white balance. Pull the slider to the left to cool down the image (add blue) and to the right to warm it up (add amber).

The **Tint** slider helps you to fine-tune the temperature setting. Slide left to add magenta and right to add green. This slider can neutralize any color cast that remains after making an adjustment to the temperature setting.

The **Eyedropper** is similar to an Auto white balance setting, but the eyedropper offers a little more control. Click this button and then mouse the cursor over a neutral grey or white area in the image to automatically adjust the color temperature. Click this button as many times as you need to get the effect right. When you're finished, click the X on the dialog bar at the bottom.

**Figure 7-20**  *Use the bottom three tools in the Adjust tab to achieve a natural look in your photos.*

**Figure 7-21**  *Use the Eyedropper to select a neutral area and set your white balance.*

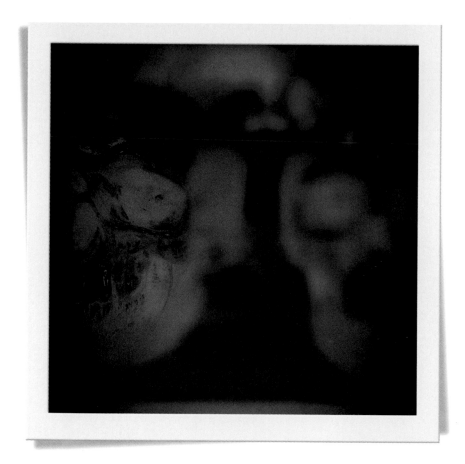

# Chapter 8

## Share Your iPhone Photos and Videos

A great thing about taking pictures and videos with your iPhone is the ease with which you can share them with friends and family. It only takes seconds—and a click of a button—to send a photo halfway around the world.

You can also upload photos to your favorite photo sharing or social networking Web sites, such as Flickr, Facebook and YouTube.

*Figure 8-1 Eventually you will need to download your photos to your computer.*

# Download your Photos and Videos

At some point in time, you're going to want to transfer your photos and videos from your iPhone to your computer—either to free up space, edit with software on your computer, or to just back them up.

Downloading your images from the iPhone can vary depending on which computer platform and operating system you use and which software you have installed.

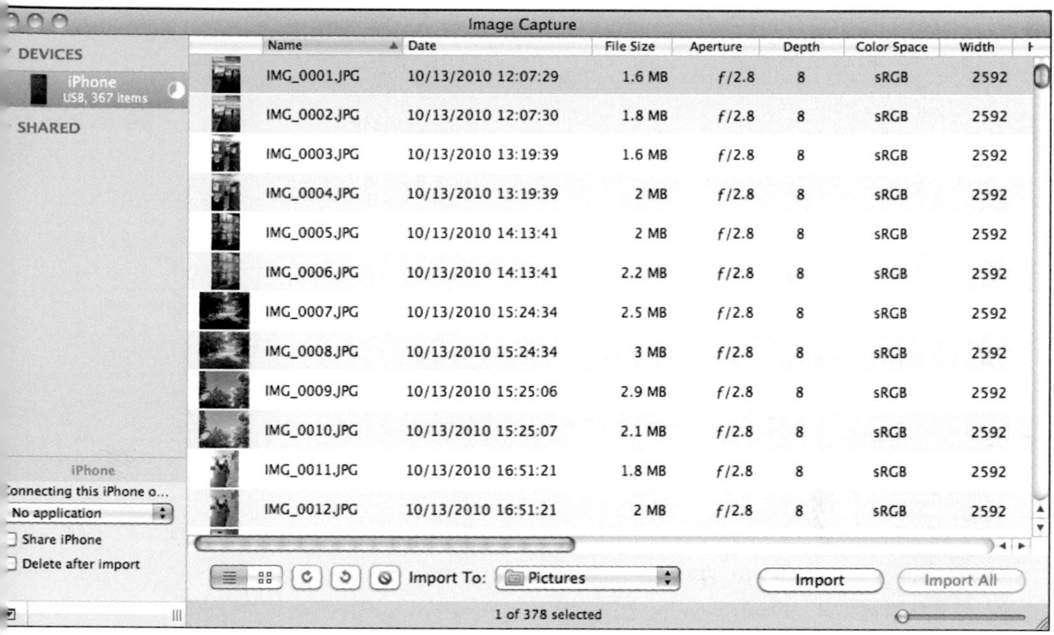

| Name | ▲ | Date | File Size | Aperture | Depth | Color Space | Width | F |
|------|---|------|-----------|----------|-------|-------------|-------|---|
| IMG_0001.JPG | | 10/13/2010 12:07:29 | 1.6 MB | f/2.8 | 8 | sRGB | 2592 | |
| IMG_0002.JPG | | 10/13/2010 12:07:30 | 1.8 MB | f/2.8 | 8 | sRGB | 2592 | |
| IMG_0003.JPG | | 10/13/2010 13:19:39 | 1.6 MB | f/2.8 | 8 | sRGB | 2592 | |
| IMG_0004.JPG | | 10/13/2010 13:19:39 | 2 MB | f/2.8 | 8 | sRGB | 2592 | |
| IMG_0005.JPG | | 10/13/2010 14:13:41 | 2 MB | f/2.8 | 8 | sRGB | 2592 | |
| IMG_0006.JPG | | 10/13/2010 14:13:41 | 2.2 MB | f/2.8 | 8 | sRGB | 2592 | |
| IMG_0007.JPG | | 10/13/2010 15:24:34 | 2.5 MB | f/2.8 | 8 | sRGB | 2592 | |
| IMG_0008.JPG | | 10/13/2010 15:24:34 | 3 MB | f/2.8 | 8 | sRGB | 2592 | |
| IMG_0009.JPG | | 10/13/2010 15:25:06 | 2.9 MB | f/2.8 | 8 | sRGB | 2592 | |
| IMG_0010.JPG | | 10/13/2010 15:25:07 | 2.1 MB | f/2.8 | 8 | sRGB | 2592 | |
| IMG_0011.JPG | | 10/13/2010 16:51:21 | 1.8 MB | f/2.8 | 8 | sRGB | 2592 | |
| IMG_0012.JPG | | 10/13/2010 16:51:21 | 2 MB | f/2.8 | 8 | sRGB | 2592 | |

DEVICES

iPhone
USB, 367 items

SHARED

iPhone
Connecting this iPhone o...
No application

Share iPhone
Delete after import

Import To:  Pictures        Import    Import All

1 of 378 selected

*Figure 8-2* *Image Capture is the easiest way to transfer your images from your iPhone to your Mac.*

# OS X

For those of you using Apple computers with OS X, the easiest way to transfer images from your iPhone to your computer is to use the Image Capture software. This is included with most versions of OS X (10.4 and up). Find it in the Applications folder and set the program to open whenever a device is attached in the Preferences menu.

Once Image Capture is up and running and the iPhone is connected, a dialog box is displayed that looks similar to a Finder window. Click on "iPhone" in the Devices list. All images from your Camera Roll will be displayed. You can then drag and drop your images to whatever folder you want.

Another option is to open iPhoto and connect your iPhone. When the iPhoto browser opens, you can select the images that you want imported. This option allows you to delete images from your phone after you import them.

I myself prefer to use Image Capture, because it's quick and easy.

**Figure 8-3** *Simply drag and drop your images from your iPhone to your PC.*

# Windows

Downloading your iPhone images to a PC is super easy. When you connect the iPhone to your PC, it will show up in the Explorer window as a USB device. Simply click on the icon; the files will appear in the window. You can then drag and drop to a folder of your choice.

If for some reason your iPhone isn't showing up as a USB device, use the Scanner and Camera Wizard to download your images. First go to the Start menu; select All Programs > Accessories > Scanner and Camera Wizard. Your iPhone should then show up as one of the available devices. The Wizard will then walk you through the steps.

.ıl. AT&T 3G     1:09 AM     50% 🔋

Camera Roll    **388 of 401**

*Figure 8-4* *The Play button starts the slideshow.*

Send Photos Button

# Play a Slideshow

Show off your photography work to your friends … right on your iPhone … with a slideshow. The slideshow plays images with a professional-looking fade-to-black dissolve. Here's how:

1. **Tap the Photos app.**

2. **Select an album** by tapping on it. Thumbnails are displayed.

3. **Select a photo** to start the show.

4. **Press the Play button.**

5. **Manage the Show.** The iPhone automatically displays each photo for about two seconds before dissolving into the next photo. You can swipe to the left to move on to the next photo or swipe to the right to go back to the previous photo. Just tap the Play button again when you have swiped to the next photo and wish to resume the slideshow's auto display.

# E-Mail & MMS

Sending photos to your friends or family in an e-mail or MMS (Multi-Media MeSsage) couldn't be easier. The iPhone makes it all very simple. Follow these easy steps:

1. **Tap the Photos app.** The icon is blue with a sunflower on it. Tapping it brings up your photo albums. There are two types of albums you will have here: Your camera roll and a photo library. The photo library can also contain multiple albums, and these all come from your computer during the sync process if you choose. You can create and select a folder to sync to your iPhone in iTunes under the Photos tab (when your iPhone is selected). The Camera Roll contains photos taken with the iPhone camera, any screenshots and pictures saved from Safari or e-mails.

2. **Select an album.** Choose the album that contains the picture you want to select and tap on it. Thumbnails are displayed.

3. **Select a photo.** Tap a photo to view it full size. You can swipe left or right to scroll through the images in the selected album. When you find the picture you want, tap the Send Photos button in the bottom left corner. This displays a pop-up menu.

4. **Select "Email Photo" or "MMS."** Enter the recipient's e-mail address for e-mail or phone number for MMS. You can also enter text to accompany the photo.

5. **Tap Send.** You're done!

You can also send multiple photos in e-mail or MMS. Just open the Photos app and select the album that contains the picture(s) you want to share. Then:

1. **Tap the Send Photos button**, which appears in the top right corner (below the battery icon) when thumbnails are displayed.

2. **Select photos.** Tap the photos you wish to send. You can select up to five photos for e-mail and up to nine for MMS.

3. **Tap the Share button.** Three buttons will then appear at the bottom of the screen: Share, Copy and Delete. Tap "Share" to access a pop-up menu.

4. **Select "Email Photo" or "MMS"** and enter the recipient's e-mail address for e-mail or phone number for MMS. You can also enter text to accompany the photo.

5. **Tap Send.**

Be aware that to send photos through e-mail on your iPhone, you must have an active e-mail account and you must have your e-mail account set up on your iPhone. To send MMS, you need a data plan.

Send Photos Button

*Figure 8-5* *The Send Photos button whisks away*
*your image file and sends it to your recipient.*

# Upload Photos and Video to Facebook

Facebook is the most popular social networking site on the Internet, and it's a great platform for sharing your photos and videos with friends, family, co-workers and others. Uploading your photos and videos from your iPhone to Facebook is a snap.

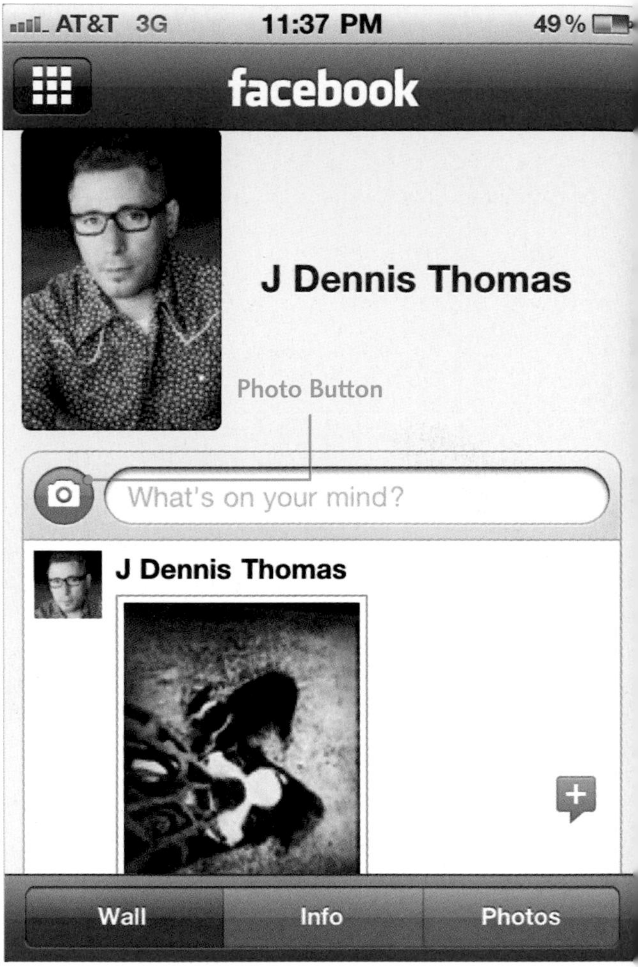

Just open the Facebook app on the iPhone and go to your Profile page. Click on the Photo button next to the Status Update box. A pop-up box appears with two choices: "Take Photo" / "Take Video" or "Choose From Library."

Selecting "Take Photo" will bring up the camera screen; "Choose From Library" will deliver the Photo Albums menu.

Now, select your preferred option. Either take a photo or select one from an album.

*Figure 8-6 The Facebook photo button allows you to choose to take a new photo or select one from your photo library.*

When you take a picture, you'll see two options: "Retake" or "Use." When you take a picture you like, tap "Use." Another menu appears at the bottom of the screen; it's the same menu that appears right after you select a picture from the album.

Tap the center of the screen to enter a caption and then tap the Upload button. The photo or video will appear on your wall within a few seconds.

After your photo is posted on your wall, you can tap on it to view full size. Tapping the Send Photo button brings up a pop-up menu with some options that apply to Facebook only.

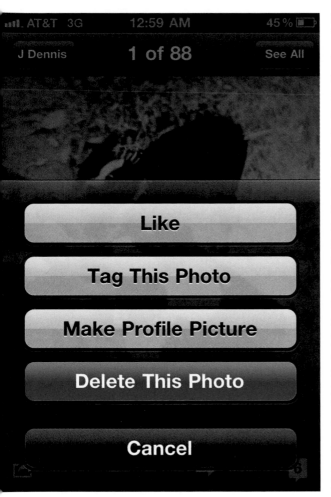

Like

Tag This Photo

Make Profile Picture

Delete This Photo

Cancel

*Figure 8-7  Here is the Facebook photo options menu.*

**Like**. Tap the Like button to "like" the photo.

**Tag this Photo**. Tap here and then tap on people or things in the photo to tag them. You can tag your Facebook friends or simply type in the name of a person or thing.

**Make Profile Picture**. This sets the selected picture as your default profile picture. You can use your fingers to crop the image to fit or to crop out any unwanted areas.

**Delete this Photo**. Tapping this button deletes the picture from your Facebook profile. If you selected the photo from a photo album, it will remain in the photo album but not on Facebook. If you selected the Take Photo option, the picture will be deleted altogether.

**Cancel**. This cancels out any options you've selected and leaves everything unchanged.

# Send Photos and Video to Flickr

If you're more into sharing your images and less into social networking, Flickr is a great site. It does have its social networking aspects to it though. There are groups on Flickr that are dedicated to all kinds of photography, including iPhone photos, and groups dedicated to specific iPhone apps, such as Hipstamatic, Plastic Bullet, Diptic and more.

To upload your photos and video to Flickr, you'll need to create an account (if you don't already have one). You also need to upload the Flickr app to your iPhone. Once you've done these two things, you can get on with the uploading process:

1. Open the Flickr app. Tap the app to open it. If it's your first time accessing the account from your iPhone, you'll have to sign in.

2. Click the Upload button. This button is located at the top right side of the screen (under the battery icon). A pop-up box appears with two choices: "Take Photo/

Flickr Upload Button

Figure 8-8 *The Flickr upload button provides the option to shoot a new photo or video or to browse your photo library to select a file to share.*

Video" or "Choose From Library." Select "Take Photo" to access the camera screen; "Choose from Library" brings up the Photo Albums menu.

3. Select your preferred option and then snap a photo or select one from an album. When you take a picture, you'll see two options: "Retake" or "Use." When you have a picture you like, tap to select it or tap "Use." The Details menu appears.

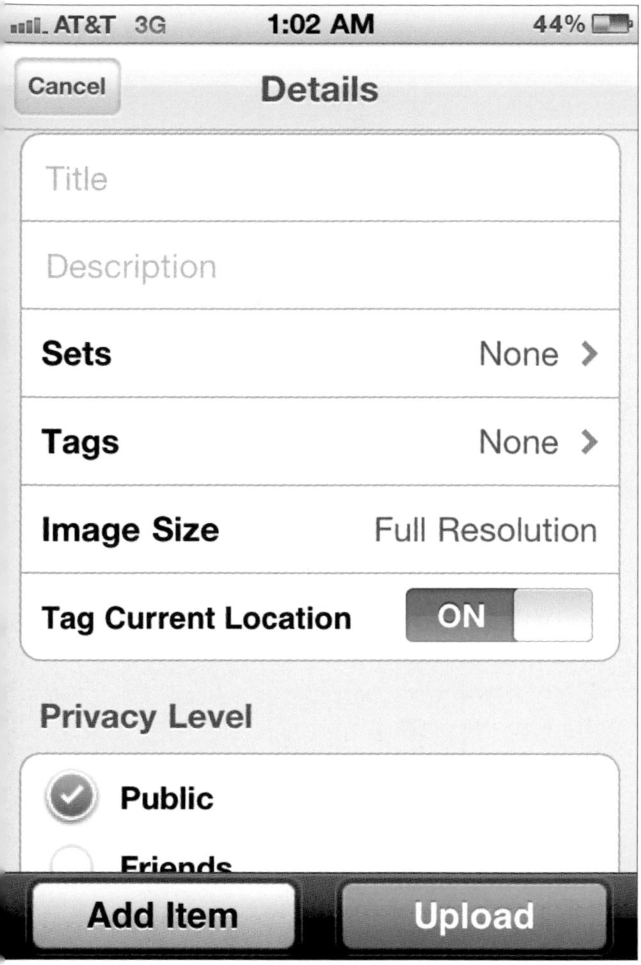

| ıılı. AT&T  3G | 1:02 AM | 44% 🔋 |
|---|---|---|

| Cancel | **Details** | |

Title

Description

| **Sets** | None 〉 |
|---|---|

| **Tags** | None 〉 |
|---|---|

| **Image Size** | Full Resolution |
|---|---|

| **Tag Current Location** | ON |
|---|---|

**Privacy Level**

✓ **Public**

◯ **Friends**

| **Add Item** | **Upload** |
|---|---|

**Figure 8-9** *You can add a wide range of information about your file with the Flickr photo Details menu.*

4. Enter the photo details—a title and description. You can add the photo to an existing set of images or create a new set. You can also add tags or create new tags and change the image size from full resolution to medium (for faster uploads). You can choose to add location information or not, and you can also specify who can see the photo (public, friends, family, friends & family, or no one: private).

5. Tap Upload to add the picture to your Flickr Photostream. If you have additional photos to add, click the Add Item button and repeat Step 4 for each additional image.

If you are a Twitter user as well, you can simultaneously tweet your photos by going to **http://www.flickr.com/account/blogs/add/twitter.**

# Upload Videos to YouTube

If you're a YouTube user, uploading videos straight from your iPhone is quick and easy. Just follow these steps:

1. **Tap the Photos app**.

2. **Select an album**. Choose the album that contains the video you want to select and tap on it. Thumbnails are displayed.

3. **Select a photo**. Tap the video thumbnail to view it full size. You can swipe left or right to scroll through the images in the selected album. When you find the file you want to share, tap the Send Photos button in the bottom left corner. This displays a pop-up menu.

4. **Select "Send to YouTube."** If this is your first time sending a video from your phone, you'll have to sign in with your username and password. When you sign in, you'll see the Publish Video screen.

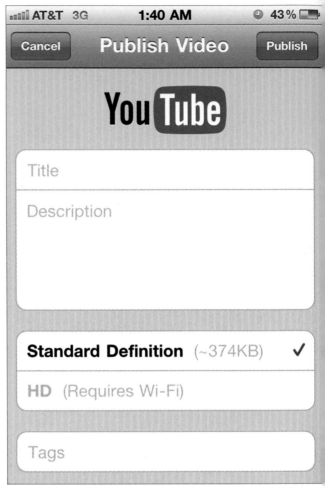

*Figure 8-10* *Use this screen to enter the video information before publishing to YouTube.*

5. **Enter the video info**. Type in the title, description, tags, etc…

6. **Tap Publish**. Your video will soon appear on YouTube for your friends and family to watch.

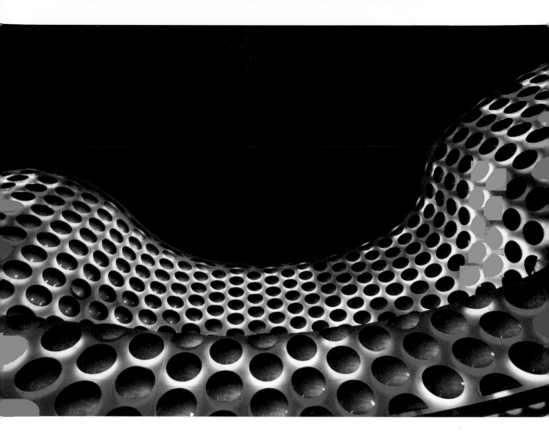

# Chapter 9

## Accessories

Due to the wild popularity of the iPhone as a camera, quite a few accessories have been designed for iPhone photography. There are lenses, tripod mounts and more. And while some of these accessories cost just a few bucks; some cost more than $200.

# Owle Bubo

Available for the iPhone 3Gs and 4G, this is one serious piece of equipment. It's probably the most advanced accessory that's made for the iPhone.

To start, the Owle Bubo is made of solid aluminum and has a wide-angle lens that also allows you to focus up-close for macro shots. The lens promises to increase the quality of your iPhone photos and video. But if that's not enough, the lens also has front threads that allow you to screw in additional filters and lenses for added versatility.

Owle Bubo also offers an adjustable microphone that delivers higher quality audio than you can get with the built-in mic of the iPhone itself. And the Bubo's cold-shoe attachment allows you to attach lighting accessories—the kind that are normally used on DSLR video cameras to aid in low-light photo and videography.

And last but not least, the Owle Bubo has threaded sockets on all four sides so you can attach the device to a tripod for stability.

This is a great accessory for the serious blogger. You can get it straight from Owle at **http://www.wantowle.com/**.

**Figure 9-1** *The Owle Bubo is a perfect accessory for the blogger covering red carpet events.*

*Figure 9-2* *The Griffin Clarifi gives you instant access to a macro lens.*

# Griffin Clarifi

The Griffin Clarifi is a protective case that has a built-in lens that enables close-up focusing for cool macro shots. The lens slides right out of the way, so you can easily use the standard iPhone lens for normal photography.

At $35, this case isn't much more expensive than a standard protective case. The Griffin Clarifi is available at most places that sell Griffin accessories, including the Apple Store and Best Buy.

*Figure 9-3* *A tripod makes your low-light images nice and sharp.*

# Gary Fong Tripod Adapter

This is a simple little device that clips around your iPhone. It has a threaded socket you can use to attach your iPhone to a tripod. Doing so will stabilize your iPhone for shooting photos in low light and make your videos steady ... free of the jitters that can show up when holding the iPhone in your hand while shooting.

You can order this and other iPhone accessories straight from **http://GaryFong.com**.

*Figure 9-4* *You can use the Gorillamobile to attach your iPhone to just about anything.*

## Joby Gorillamobile

The Gorillamobile is a very versatile accessory. It comes as a functional bumper case that has an attachable flexible tripod. Attach the Gorillamobile to all kinds of objects for the ultimate in tripod versatility.

Joby products are available at better camera stores and at **http://joby.com**.

**Figure 9-5** *The soft focus lens adds a cool blur to your photos.*

# Kikkerland Jelly Lenses

These are probably the most affordable accessories for an iPhone camera that I've found. The Kikkerland Jelly Lenses are inexpensive plastic lenses that stick right over the iPhone lens using a non-adhesive silicon rubber. Presumably, this is where the "jelly" moniker originates.

There are a number of different lenses: close-up, wide-angle, starburst, kaleidoscope, stretch, soft focus and a few others.

I own the close-up lens, and I really like it. This lens allows you to get really close macro shots. I also have the wide-angle lens. I use this one less frequently, but it gives a really cool wide-angle distortion. There is a little vignetting, but it kinda adds to the lo-fi effect.

*Figure 9-6* *Take cool art deco pictures with your cool art deco Quattro case.*

# Factron Quattro Case

The Factron Quattro Case is packed with features ... and targeted for the fashionable crowd. The Quattro is a brushed aluminum nouveau art-deco case.

The Quattro isn't strictly designed for photography, but it has a screw-mount, so you can add lenses for an additional cost. The lenses include a fisheye, a wide-angle and a close-up attachment.

The case starts out at around $200 and the lenses go for $15-$50 more--not cheap. But you will definitely have the fanciest iPhone in the house with this accessory!

These things aren't easy to find though. Check **http://www.geekstuff4u.com** for availability.

# Index

## A

accessories
    Factron Quattro Case, 176
    Gary Fong tripod adapter, 173
    Griffin Clarifi case, 34, 172
    Joby Gorillamobile, 174
    Kikkerland Jelly Lenses, 17, 34, 175
    Owle Bubo, 170–171
    telephoto lens, 40
    tripods, 26, 50
Adjust tab (iPhoto)
    about, 146–147
    details adjustments using, 152–153
    Levels tool, 148–149
    tonality adjustments using, 150–151
adjustment layers (Photoshop Elements)
    Hue and Saturation adjustments, 130–131
    Levels adjustment, 126–129
    nondestructive editing using, 125
    for retouching, 132
Adobe. *See also* Photoshop Elements
    Photoshop, 9, 31
    Photoshop Express app, 60–61, 119
Antique effect, 144
anti-shake feature, apps with, 74, 75
aperture of iPhone camera, 10
apps
    Camera Bag, 2, 35, 86–87
    Camera Plus, 74
    Camera Plus Pro, 74
    ClassicTOY, 80–81
    Cross Process, 98–99
    Darkroom, 26, 94–95
    Dash of Color, 68–69
    Diptic, 66–67
    Facebook, 164–165
    FilterFX for Free, 70–71
    Flickr, 166–167
    Golden Hour, 56
    Gorillacam, 75
    Helga, 2
    Hipstamatic, 78–79
    iMovie, 117
    Impression, 88
    Infinicam, 92–93
    Iron Camera, 76–77
    LoFi, 64–65
    moreLomo, 53, 82–83
    moreMono (Red Edition), 84–85
    MovieFX for Free, 72–73
    PanoLab, 100–101
    Photo Tidy, 9
    Photos, 161–163, 168
    Photoshop Express, 60–61, 119
    Plastic Bullet, 3, 33, 62–63
    Pro HDR, 55
    Retro Camera, 96–97
    RetroCamera, 89
    ShakeItPhoto, 90–91
    Sloppy Borders, 32
architecture, shooting, 31

## B

background noise in video, 113
background of images, 23, 109
backlit subjects
    blocking the light source, 52
    flare with, 52, 53
    flash for, 4
    in photos, avoiding, 45
    in video, avoiding, 115
Backside Illumination (BSI), 6, 7
B&W effect, 144
beauty in everyday objects, 21
black-and-white images
    B&W effect for, 144
    Camera Plus app for, 74
    Dash of Color app for, 68
    Photoshop Elements for, 130
    Plastic Bullet app for, 62
blur
    from camera movement, avoiding, 26, 34, 50–51, 94–95, 105
    Edge Blur effect, 144
    Gaussian blur effect, 134
    Kikkerland Jelly Lenses for soft focus, 175
    lens, Plastic Bullet app for, 62
    from low light, 50

Boost effect, 144
borders or frames
  Infinicam app for, 92–93
  iPhoto effects for, 144
  Photoshop Express for, 60–61
  Plastic Bullet app for, 62
  RetroCamera app for, 89
  Sloppy Borders app for, 32
buildings, shooting, 31
burst shooting, app for, 75

## C

Camera Bag app, 2, 35, 86–87
camera movement
  apps with anti-shake feature, 74, 75
  Darkroom app for avoiding, 26, 94–95
  holding the camera steady, 26, 50, 105
  with macro shots, 34
  tripod for reducing, 26, 50, 105
Camera Plus app, 74
Camera Plus Pro app, 74
cameras. *See also* iPhone camera; toy camera
  iPhone compared to DSLR or compact, 1, 15
  point-and-shoot, 3
candid shots, 32
cases
  Factron Quattro Case, 176
  Griffin Clarify, 34, 172
  Owle Bubo, 170–171
children, shooting videos of, 110
ClassicTOY app, 80–81
close-up and macro photography
  examples, 17, 28, 34
  for filling the frame, 28
  guidelines for, 34
  holding the camera steady, 34
  lenses for, 17, 34, 170, 172, 175, 176
  minimum focus distance, 17
  video, framing heads for, 108
cluttered photos, avoiding, 22, 29
collages, apps for, 64, 66–67
color temperature. *See* white balance
color wheel, 24
colors. *See also* saturation
  bright and bold, for great images, 24
  complementary, 24

correcting in Photoshop Elements, 129
Cross Process app filters for, 98–99
Dash of Color app for, 68–69
Effects tab adjustments in iPhoto, 142–143
at golden hour, 56
hue adjustment in Photoshop Elements, 130–131
shifts with cross processing, 64, 65
at sunrise and sunset, 38
white balance, 16, 120, 129, 154–155
compact cameras, 1, 3, 15
complementary colors, 24
composite images, apps for, 64, 66–67
composition. *See also* cropping
  filling the frame, 28
  framing heads in video, 108
  gridlines for, 74, 75
  keeping simple, 22
  as key for iPhone photography, 3
  lines in, 25
  patterns in, 25
  portrait versus landscape orientation, 27
  Rule of Thirds for, 29, 36, 104
  sense of place in, 23
  textures in, 25
  vanishing point for, 30
  of video, 104
computer, downloading to, 158–160
continuous shooting, app for, 75
contrast
  adjusting with iPhoto, 142, 144, 148, 150
  adjusting with Photoshop Express, 60–61
  high, handling, 54–55
Contrast effect, 142
Cooler effect, 142
copyrighting photos, app for, 88
countdown timer, 74
crooked images, straightening, 124, 138
cropping
  Camera Plus app for, 74
  digital zoom versus, 14
  Infinicam app for, 93
  iPhoto for, 138
  Photoshop Elements for, 123
  Photoshop Express for, 60–61
Cross Process app, 98–99

cross processing
   apps simulating, 62, 64–65, 98–99
   defined, 64, 98

**D**
Darken effect, 142
Darkroom app, 26, 94–95
Dash of Color app, 68–69
depth
   front lighting diminishing, 58
   side lighting emphasizing, 48
   vanishing point emphasizing, 30
depth of field
   background issues for deep field, 23
   defined, 10
   examples illustrating, 10, 11
   focus distance for controlling, 10, 11
   shallow, simulating, 134
diffused (soft) light, 42, 43
diffusing sunlight, 47
digital noise, 8–9, 152
digital zoom, 4, 14, 105
Diptic app, 66–67
direction of light, 41
downloading to your computer, 158–160
DSLR cameras, 1, 15
dynamic images
   capturing action for, 32
   complementary colors for, 24
   patterns for, 25
   Rule of Thirds for, 29
   side lighting for, 48
   vanishing point for, 30
dynamic range, 15

**E**
Edge Blur effect, 144
editing photos. See iPhoto; Photoshop
   Elements; post-processing
editing video
   iMovie app for, 117
   trimming in the iPhone, 116
effects and filters. See also apps; saturation
   cross processing, 62, 64
   Effects tab (iPhoto), 140–145
   FudgeCam effect, 96

Helga effect, 2, 86
Little Orange Box effect, 96, 97
Lomo effect, 86
for movie look, 72–73
Photoshop Express for, 60
Polaroid effect, 86, 87
Sepia effect, 70
Vintage filter, 71
Effects tab (iPhoto)
   about, 140–141
   Antique effect, 144
   B&W effect, 144
   Boost effect, 144
   Contrast effect, 142
   Cooler effect, 142
   Darken effect, 142
   Edge Blur effect, 144
   Fade effect, 144
   Lighten effect, 142
   Matte effect, 144
   reverting to original, 144
   Saturate effect, 142
   Sepia effect, 144
   Vignette effect, 144
   Warmer effect, 142
Elements. See Photoshop Elements
e-mailing photos, 93, 162–163
Enhance button (iPhoto), 138
everyday subjects, 21
exposure adjustment
   iPhoto for, 150
   Photoshop Express for, 60–61

**F**
Facebook app, 164–165
Facebook, uploading photos or videos to, 60,
   79, 164–165
faces in video, framing, 108
Factron Quattro Case, 176
Fade effect, 144
filling the frame, 28
film simulations. See also toy camera
   cross processing, 62, 64–65, 98–99
   with Hipstamatic app, 78
   Polaroid, 86, 87, 90–91
   Retro Camera app for, 96

with RetroCamera app, 89
FilterFX for Free app, 70–71
filters. *See* effects and filters
fisheye lens, 176
Fix Red-Eye feature (iPhoto), 138
flare
    from back lighting, 52, 53
    Plastic Bullet app for, 63
flash, 4, 5
Flickr app, 166–167
    Flickr, uploading photos or videos to, 63, 79, 166–167
focus
    close-focus capabilities, 34
    depth of field's relationship to, 10
    minimum focus distance, 17
    selective, for video, 107
    selective, with iPhone 4 and 3Gs, 3, 4
frames. *See* borders or frames
front lighting, 58, 114
FudgeCam effect, 96
Full Edit Mode (Photoshop Elements), 122
Full Screen mode (iPhoto), 136–137

## G

Gary Fong tripod adapter, 173
Gaussian blur effect, 134
golden hour, 56–57. *See also* sunrise and sunset photos
Golden Hour app, 56
Gorillacam app, 75
Gorillamobile (Joby), 174
Gradient tool (Photoshop Elements), 134
gridlines for composition, 74, 75
Griffin Clarifi case, 34, 172
guidelines for shooting
    backgrounds, 23
    breaking the rules, 19
    buildings and architecture, 31
    candid shots, 32
    close-up and macro photography, 34
    color, 24
    filling the frame, 28
    holding the camera steady, 26, 50, 105
    keep it simple, 22
    landscapes, 36

lines, patterns, and textures, 25
pets, 34
portrait versus landscape orientation, 27
Rule of Thirds, 29, 36, 104
sunrise and sunset photos, 38–39
travel photography, 37
ultra-normal subjects, 21
unusual subjects, 20
vanishing point use, 30
weather, 33
wildlife, 40

## H

hard light, 44–45
heads in video, framing, 108
Helga effect, 2, 86
high contrast, 54–55
highlights
    adjusting with iPhoto, 142, 152
    adjusting with Photoshop Elements, 120, 128
    blown-out, 15, 54
    dynamic range issues for, 15
    warm, Antique effect for, 144
Hipstamatic app, 78–79
histogram
    iPhoto, 148
    Photoshop Elements, 128
Holga toy camera, 2
horizon, straightening, 124, 138
Hue and Saturation adjustments (Photoshop Elements), 130–131

## I

Image Capture (OS X), 159
image-editing tools. *See* iPhoto; Photoshop Elements; post-processing
iMovie app, 117
Impression app, 88
indoor lighting, 42, 43. *See also* low light
Infinicam app, 92–93
iOS 4. *See also* iPhone 3G; iPhone 3Gs; iPhone 4
    digital zoom with, 4, 14
    HDR feature with 4.1, 55
    selective focus with, 3, 4
iPhone 3G

digital zoom with, 4, 14
HDR feature with, 55
low-light performance of, 6, 8
maximum print size with, 18
megapixels with, 6, 18
minimum focus distance of, 17
resolution of, 6, 18
sensor of, 18
shutter lag on, 12
iPhone 3Gs
close-focus capability of, 34
digital zoom with, 4, 14
focus point selection with, 3, 4
HDR feature with, 55
low-light performance of, 6, 8
maximum print size with, 18
megapixels with, 6, 18
minimum focus distance of, 17
resolution of, 6, 18
sensor of, 18
shutter lag improved on, 12
iPhone 4
BSI technology with, 6
close-focus capability of, 34
digital zoom with, 4, 14
focus point selection with, 3, 4
HDR feature with, 55
LED flash with, 4
low-light performance of, 6
maximum print size with, 18
megapixels with, 6, 18
minimum focus distance of, 17
resolution of, 6, 18
sensor of, 6, 18
shutter lag improved on, 12
iPhone camera
aperture of, 10
close-focus capabilities, 34
depth of field with, 10–11
digital zoom with, 6, 14
dynamic range of, 15
holding steady, 26, 50, 105
iOS 4 upgrades to, 4, 14
limitations of, 2, 3
low-light performance of, 6–9
maximum print sizes with, 18

minimum focus distances of, 17
as point-and-shoot camera, 3
popularity of, 1
quality of, 1
resolution of, 6
sensor of, 6
shutter lag with, 12–13
as "toy camera," 2
white balance adjustment by, 16
iPhone original
low-light performance of, 6, 8
maximum print size with, 18
megapixels with, 6, 18
minimum focus distance of, 17
resolution of, 6, 18
sensor of, 18
shutter lag on, 12
iPhoto. See also post-processing
Adjust tab, 146–155
all digital photos editable with, 135
color adjustments using, 142–143
described, 135
digital zoom versus cropping in, 14
digital zoom versus cropping with, 14
Edit button, 136
Effects tab, 140–145
Full Screen mode, 136–137
histogram, 148
Levels tool, 148–149
menu palette, 136
noise reduction using, 9
photo effects, 144–145
Quick Fixes tab, 138–139
tonality adjustments using, 142–143, 150–151
white balance adjustment using, 154–155
Iron Camera app, 75–76

J
Joby Gorillamobile, 174

K
kaleidoscope lens, 175
kids, shooting videos of, 110
Kikkerland Jelly Lenses, 17, 34, 175

# L

landscape orientation, 27, 138
landscapes
    guidelines for shooting, 36
    portrait orientation for, 27
LED flash, 4, 5
lenses
    aperture of iPhone camera, 10
    with Factron Quattro Case, 176
    with Griffin Clarifi case, 34, 172
    Hipstamatic app simulating, 78
    Kikkerland Jelly Lenses, 17, 34, 175
    for macro shots, 17, 34, 170, 172, 175, 176
    with Owle Bubo, 170
    quality of iPhone camera, 2
    telephoto, 40
    wide-angle, 170, 175, 176
Levels adjustment (Photoshop Elements)
    adjustment layer for, 126
    color correction using, 129
    histogram in dialog box, 128
    overview, 126–127
Levels tool (iPhoto), 148–149
light and lighting. See also low light
    backlit subjects, 4, 45, 52–53, 115
    capturing the weather, 33
    direction of, 41
    dynamic range of, 15
    flash, 4, 5
    front, 58, 114
    fundamental importance of, 41
    golden hour, 56–57
    hard, 44–45
    high contrast, 54–55
    indoor, 42, 43
    for landscapes, 36
    outdoor, 46–47
    Owle Bubo for attaching accessories, 170
    quality of, 41
    side, 48–49
    soft or diffused, 42
    sunrise and sunset photos, 38–39
    for video, 114
    white balance of, 16
light leak simulation, app for, 62

Lighten effect, 142
lines for composition, 25
Little Orange Box effect, 96, 97
location
    giving photos a sense of, 23
    for "wildlife" shots, 40
LoFi app, 64–65
Lomo effect, 2
Lomo toy camera, 2
low light. See also light and lighting
    blur with, avoiding, 26, 50–51
    blurred images from, 50
    BSI technology for, 6, 7
    Darkroom app for shooting in, 26, 94–95
    digital noise with, 8
    guidelines for shooting in, 50–51
    resolution and sensor size affecting, 6
    tripod for, 26, 50, 173
luminosity, adjusting
    iPhoto for, 142, 148
    Photoshop Elements for, 128

# M

macro photography. See close-up and macro photography
Macs, downloading to, 159
magnifying lens for close-ups, 34
Matte effect, 144
megapixels. See also resolution
    calculation of, 18
    with iPhone 3Gs, 6, 18
    with iPhone 4, 6, 18
    with iPhone original and 3G, 6, 18
    print size limited by, 18
    sensor size not changed with additional, 6
mergers in backgrounds, avoiding, 23, 109
microphone for video, 113, 170
mid-tones, adjusting
    iPhoto for, 142, 152
    Photoshop Elements for, 128
minimum focus distance
    defined, 17
    of iPhone models, 17
    Kikkerland Jelly Lenses for reducing, 17, 34, 175
MMS (Multi-Media MeSsage), sending photos via, 162–163

monochrome images. *See also* black-and-white images
  moreMono (Red Edition) for, 84–85
  Photoshop Elements for, 130
moreLomo app, 53, 82–83
moreMono (Red Edition) app, 84–85
MovieFX for Free app, 72–73
music for video, 117

**N**

noise, digital, 8–9, 152
noise when recording video, 113

**O**

orientation
  changing in iPhoto, 138
  landscape versus portrait, 27
OS X, downloading to, 159
outdoor lighting. *See also* low light; sunrise and sunset photos
  backlit subjects, 4, 45, 52–53, 115
  cloudy, as soft light, 42, 46
  diffusing sunlight, 47
  direct sunlight, as hard light, 44–45
  front lighting, 58, 114
  high contrast, 54–55
  in shade, 42, 46
  side lighting, 48–49
  soft light, 42
  for video, 114
Owle Bubo, 170–171

**P**

panning, 106
PanoLab app for panoramas, 100–101
patterns in photos, 25
PCs, downloading to, 160
perspective
  for shooting buildings, 31
  for video, 110
pets
  photos of, 34
  videos of, 110
Photo Tidy app, 9
Photos app
  e-mailing photos, 162–163
  playing a slideshow, 161
  sending photos by MMS, 162–163
  uploading videos to YouTube, 168
Photoshop
  for building and architecture shots, 31
  noise reduction using, 9
Photoshop Elements. *See also* post-processing
  adjustment layers, 125
  boosting saturation with, 120
  color correction, 129
  cropping with, 123
  described, 119
  digital zoom versus cropping in, 14
  digital zoom versus cropping with, 14
  free 30-day trial of, 119
  Full Edit Mode, 122
  highlights adjustment using, 120, 128
  histogram, 128
  Hue and Saturation adjustments, 130–131
  Levels adjustment, 126–129
  Lighting option, 120
  mid-tones adjustment using, 128
  nondestructive editing using, 122, 125
  Quick Fix Mode, 120–121
  retouching using, 132–133
  shadows adjustment using, 120, 128
  for shallow depth of field simulation, 134
  sharpening using, 120
  Smart Fix, 120
  Straighten tool, 124
  white balance adjustment using, 120, 129
Photoshop Express app, 60–61, 119
Photoshop.com, uploading photos to, 60
place
  giving photos a sense of, 23
  for "wildlife" shots, 40
planning video shots, 111
Plastic Bullet app, 3, 33, 62–63
playing a slideshow, 161
point-and-shoot cameras, 3. *See also* iPhone camera
Polaroid simulation
  Camera Bag Polaroid effect for, 86, 87
  ShakeItPhoto app for, 90–91
portrait orientation, 27, 138

portraits
    candid, 32
    flash for backlit subjects, 4
    landscape orientation for, 27
post-processing. *See also* iPhoto; Photoshop Elements
    for building and architecture shots, 31
    cropping, digital zoom versus, 14
    digital zoom versus cropping during, 14
    for noise reduction, 8–9
    Photoshop Express app for, 60–61, 119
    for white balance adjustment, 16
printing photos, 18
Pro HDR app, 55
publishing videos on YouTube, 168

**Q**

quality of light, 41
quality of video sound, 113
Quick Fix Mode (Photoshop Elements), 120–121
Quick Fixes tab (iPhoto), 138–139

**R**

red-eye, fixing in iPhoto, 138
resolution
    digital zoom reducing, 14
    of iPhone 3Gs, 6, 18
    of iPhone 4, 6, 18
    of iPhone original and 3G, 6, 18
    with Iron Camera app, 76
    low light and higher resolutions, 6
    of photo printers, 18
    print size limited by, 18
retouching
    iPhoto for, 138
    Photoshop Elements for, 132–133
Retro Camera app, 96–97
RetroCamera app, 89
Rotate option (iPhoto), 138
Rule of Thirds, 29, 36, 104

**S**

Saturate effect, 142
saturation. *See also* cross processing
    adjusting with iPhoto, 138, 142, 144, 150

adjusting with Photoshop Elements, 120, 130
boosted by cross processing, 64
boosting with Photoshop Express, 60–61
with moreMono (Red Edition) app, 84
Scanner and Camera Wizard (Windows), 160
S-curve for composition, 25
selective focus
    with iPhone 4 and 3Gs, 3, 4
    for video, 107
self-timer, app with, 75
sending photos and videos. *See* sharing photos and videos
sensor of iPhone camera
    BSI technology for, 6
    depth of field affected by, 10
    dynamic range of, 15
    image capturing process of, 6
    of iPhone 4 and 3Gs, 18
    of iPhone original and 3G, 18
    size not changed with additional pixels, 6
Sepia effect, 70, 144
sequence shots, video, 112
shadows
    adjusting with iPhoto, 142, 152
    adjusting with Photoshop Elements, 120, 128
    cool, Antique effect for, 144
    dynamic range issues for, 15
    high contrast, 54–55
ShakeItPhoto app, 90–91
sharing photos and videos
    downloading to computer, 158–160
    ease of, 157
    in e-mail messages, 162–163
    on Facebook, 60, 79, 164–165
    on Flickr, 63, 79, 166–167
    in MMS messages, 162–163
    on Photoshop.com, 60
    playing a slideshow, 161
    on Tumblr, 79
    on Twitter, 60
    on YouTube, 168
sharpening
    iPhoto for, 152
    Photoshop Elements for, 120
shutter lag
    defined, 12

examples illustrating issues with, 12, 13
improvements with iPhone 4 and 3Gs, 12
tip for dealing with, 12
side lighting, 48–49
simplicity
for backgrounds, 23
filling the frame for, 28
importance of, 22
"Sin City" filter, 72
slideshow, playing, 161
Sloppy Borders app, 32
sneaker zoom, 105
soft focus lens, 175
soft light, 42, 43
software. See apps; specific software
sound for video
music using iMovie, 117
recording when shooting, 113
special effects. See effects and filters
sports photography, shutter lag issues for, 12
starburst lens, 175
stitching panoramic views, app for, 100–101
straightening images, 124, 138
street photography, 32
stretch lens, 175
subjects for photos
backlit, tips for, 4, 52–53
buildings and architecture, 31
complementary colors in, 24
keeping simple, 22
landscapes, 27, 36
lines, 25
mergers in backgrounds, avoiding, 23, 109
patterns, 25
pets, 34
portraits, 4, 27, 32
sense of place for, 23
simple background for, 23
textures, 25
ultra-normal, 21
unusual, 20
weather, 33
wildlife, 40
sunlight
cloudy or shade, as soft light, 42, 46
diffusing, 47
direct, as hard light, 44–45
front lighting, 58, 114
golden hour, 56–57
high contrast, 54–55
side lighting, 48–49
window light, 42, 43
sunrise and sunset photos. See also low light
golden hour, 56–57
guidelines for shooting, 38–39
landscapes, 36

T

tactile feeling, textures for, 25
tap focus feature
with iPhone 4 and 3Gs, 3, 4
for video, 107
telephoto lens accessories, 40
textures
hard light for, 45
iPhoto for emphasizing, 152
side lighting for, 48
tactile feeling from, 25
Themes for video, 117
thirds, rule of, 29, 36, 104
time-lapse photography, 75
tonality, adjusting
iPhoto for, 142–143, 150–151
Photoshop Elements for, 120
toy camera
Camera Bag app simulating, 2, 86
ClassicTOY app simulating, 80–81
fun art photos using, 2
Hipstamatic app simulating, 78–79
by Holga and Lomo, 2
iPhone camera as, 2
Iron Camera app simulating, 76
moreLomo app simulating, 82–83
Plastic Bullet app simulating, 62–63
travel photography, guidelines for, 37
trimming video in the iPhone, 116
tripod
Gary Fong adapter for, 173
Joby Gorillamobile, 174
for low light, 26, 50, 173
Owle Bubo adapter for, 170
for time-lapse photography, 75

Tumblr, uploading photos to, 79
"Twilight" filter, 73
Twitter, uploading photos to, 60

## U

ultra-normal subjects, 21
unusual subjects, 20
uploading photos and videos
    to Facebook, 60, 79, 164–165
    to Flickr, 63, 79, 166–167
    to Photoshop.com, 60
    to Tumblr, 79
    to Twitter, 60
    to YouTube, 168

## V

vanishing point, 30
vertical alignment, fixing, 124, 138
video. *See also* sharing photos and videos
    backlighting, avoiding, 115
    composition of, 104
    framing heads, 108
    front lighting for, 114
    holding the camera steady, 105
    iMovie app for editing, 117
    mergers in, avoiding, 109
    microphone for, 113, 170
    music for, 117
    panning, 106
    perspective for, 110
    of pets and kids, 110
    photographs versus, 103
    planning shots, 111
    publishing on YouTube, 168
    sequence shots, 112
    sneaker zoom for, 105
    sound recording for, 113
    tap focus feature with, 107
    Themes for, 117
    trimming in the iPhone, 116
    zooming digitally, avoiding, 105
vignetting
    moreLomo app for, 82
    Vignette effect for, 144
Vintage filter, 71

## W

Warmer effect, 142
watermark, app for, 88
weather, capturing, 33
weird subjects, 20
whip pans, 106
white balance, adjusting
    automatic by iPhone, 16
    examples illustrating, 16
    iPhoto for, 154–155
    Photoshop Elements for, 120, 129
    post-processing for, 16
wide-angle lenses, 170, 175, 176
wildlife photography, guidelines for, 40
window light, 42, 43
Windows, downloading to, 160

## X

X-pro. *See* cross processing

## Y

YouTube, uploading videos to, 168

## Z

zoom
    cropping versus zooming, 14
    digital, 4, 14, 105
    sneaker, 105
zoos, shooting at, 40